LOVE AND BLOOD

AT THE WORLD CUP WITH THE FOOTBALLERS, FANS, AND FREAKS

JAMIE TRECKER

A HARVEST ORIGINAL · HARCOURT, INC.

ORLANDO   AUSTIN   NEW YORK   SAN DIEGO   LONDON

Copyright © 2007 by Jamie Trecker

www.HarcourtBooks.com

Library of Congress Cataloging-in-Publication Data
Trecker, Jamie.
Love and blood: at the World Cup with the footballers,
fans, and freaks/Jamie Trecker.—1st ed.
p.   cm.
"A Harvest original."
Includes bibliographical references and index.
1. World Cup (Soccer) (2006: Germany)   2. Soccer teams.
3. Soccer players.   4. Soccer fans.   I. Title.
GV943.49.T74   2007
796.334'668—dc22   2007020546
ISBN 978-0-15-603098-4

Text set in Minion
Designed by Linda Lockowitz

Printed in the United States of America
First edition
A C E G I K J H F D B

For
Jerry and Janice
and
Luis and Jacqueline

CONTENTS

INTRODUCTION:
LOVE AND BLOOD

LEIPZIG (Dec 9, 2005)—It was the biggest day of the year for the sport.

No games were played—the only person who even kicked a soccer ball was Germany's national team captain, and he did it on stage to tout a new model from Adidas.

And yet over 300 million people worldwide would tune in to this small Saxon town. They'd cheer with delight or groan in agony as a supermodel and a passel of soccer celebrities pulled little balls out of fishbowls.

This was the World Cup draw, the planet's biggest lottery and the run-up for the largest show in the universe.

My job? To stand in the rain, trying to catch coaches and celebs as they entered the convention hall for the draw. Just a quick moment of your time, sir? Excuse me, coach?

João Havelange, the ex-president of the Fédération Internationale de Football Association (FIFA), stumbled out of his limo and looked, almost expectantly, at the gaggle. No one said a word; as a group, we sized him up and tossed him back to sulk into the theater. The coach of England, Sven-Göran Eriksson, pulled up. Only a few shouts came for him. Bruce

Arena and his handlers from the U.S. Soccer Federation walked past without raising an eyebrow.

No, the man everyone in the group wanted to talk to was the head coach of that world soccer power . . . *Australia*.

Guus Hiddink knew what was coming, and as soon as his car door opened he began to sprint toward the convention hall. The race was on. A hundred Asian camera crews ran to cut him off, penning him into a corner. Bouncers strained to contain reporters who lacked a quick first step, but to little avail. One enterprising Korean journalist tried to crawl between the scuffling feet with his notebook in his mouth, only to be picked up by the scruff of his jacket.

What did these poor people want? They wanted the answer to the one question that every Asian journalist, without fail, asks of anyone involved in soccer. You could be sitting at dinner, or in a press box—hell, even taking a dump—and if they know you're there, they'll ask it. This goes double for those poor ex-coaches who happened to, just once, steer a small Asian country—say South Korea—to World Cup glory.

"Mr. Hiddink, Mr. Hiddink—what do you think of the Korean team?"

As Hiddink swam through the crowd to the door, shouting over the crush in a mixture of Dutch and English while cameras worth hundreds of thousands of dollars started to hit the pavement, I had to smile.

The World Cup was back.

My first taste of what the World Cup could do came in 2002. On a hot summer day, I rode an empty train back from Jeonju, desperate for some rest. Deep circles ringed my eyes, and I had lost fifteen pounds since the World Cup kicked off.

I had been living on a diet of noodles, *anju* (loosely translated as "food for beer"), kimchi, beer, and whatever else was left lying around at the press center. I stank to high heaven and my shoulders were hunched from carrying my laptop from subway to train to bus to stadium to stairs to desk to stairs and all over again.

The USA had qualified for the quarterfinal round of the World Cup the night before by beating their archrivals Mexico. The match took place some 7,600 miles from Chicago, the home of the U.S. Soccer Federation, and given that it was 2:30 A.M. on the East Coast when the game kicked off, very few Americans even knew that the match was taking place.

But here, the sun was glaring through the smog, bright and painful, as we pulled into Seoul station. As we alighted, I began to hear voices. A lot of them. Very, very loud.

I had heard it before, many times by this point: "DAE-HAN-MIN-GUK!" or, "Go Republic!" the chant of the South Korean soccer team. But I'd never heard it quite like this.

From above, the crowd at the station looked like a giant red insect—everyone was pressed together, wearing red shirts and red scarves and red hats on top of floppy black hair. I read the next day that more than two hundred thousand people were crammed below me on the terminal floor, all sitting patiently in front of a giant television screen, awaiting kickoff, and yelling at the top of their lungs.

It was terrifying—a sound like Iron Maiden if you had them play in the main concourse at Grand Central Station with the amps up to ten, shaking the chandeliers and breaking the glass. The visceral passion of tens of thousands of South Korean soccer fans expressed in a single voice was more overwhelming than anything I'd heard on the terraces at

Ibrox, in the stands at the Kop or Old Trafford, or on the stone steps at the Azteca.

This wasn't just a group of soccer fans: This was a whole nation. I would later find out that fifteen million South Koreans—about one-third of the population of the country—had filled the streets of the capital.

At that moment, tired and frightened, I wanted to get the hell out of there.

Outside, in the stew that passed for air in Seoul, another crush was waiting in front of another massive plasma screen.

What the hell was going on?

I found myself face-to-face with a young woman, her long black hair streaked a fiery, artificial red that may well have been house paint. Her eyes were crazed, as if she didn't quite know where she was. But she knew one thing—that I wasn't wearing the communal red, red for the Republic of Korea.

She screamed full-on, in my face, as if I were an invading trooper. Then she did something even more out of character for her culture.

She flipped me off.

Both of us were startled.

The day grew weirder as it dragged on. The city lapsed into long silences after the South Korean kickoff. Then, each time a South Korean touched the ball hundreds of miles south in Daejeon, the entire city would scream, scaring the crap out of me.

Near my hotel, the park—a precious open-air greensward in that urban arrondissement—lay bare, the baby carriages and benches empty. Every building bled with red banners, and stores were open, but no one—not even the staff—was in them. Meanwhile, the massive, dizzying Tek Center, ten floors of the electronic gadgets and gizmos that had made Korea newly rich, was top-heavy with people crowding around every one of the thousands of TVs, cell phones, and computers, all tuned in to The Game.

I saw the second half from Daejeon at the COEX Press Center. As the light began to fade, I watched a gaggle of nervous Italian journalists bite their pens when the game went into extra time and their South Korean aides-de-camp roared with delight. In the 117th minute, South Korea eliminated Italy behind an incredible goal from the already wildly popular Ahn Jung-Hwan.

Seoul exploded.

Kwanghwamum Park, the downtown area where thousands had gathered for previous games, was overrun, the police unable to contain the masses. The countryside had emptied; whole towns had driven into Seoul. The city was in the midst of a full-scale riot that evening—a peaceful, happy one, but a riot no less.

Walking home that night—normally a fifteen-minute trip—took me five hours. All of Seoul seemed to be lined up on that main street, and as an American ("a blood brother," according to the South Koreans), I was repeatedly hugged, grabbed by the arm, and asked to eat and drink. I was toasted with whiskey; I was drenched in cold, sticky Hite beer; and I ate a great deal of fried food.

I don't remember getting back to my hotel, but I do remember that the next day, when I awoke to a surprisingly powerful headache, I knew something had changed. I'd just had a taste of how powerful and how exuberant the World Cup really is. Neither I, nor the nation of South Korea, would ever be the same.

The FIFA World Cup is the planet's biggest event. Not sporting event—*event,* period.

Simply put, there is nothing else like it. The Olympics would love to be it; the Super Bowl and World Series are merely pretenders to it; and only because we live in America is the World Cup not talked about in hushed, reverent tones as the pinnacle of civilized and sporting life.

I'm not joking. Husbands have mortgaged their homes to attend it. Careers are defined by it, and athletes have been murdered for fucking it up. Some countries have even declared national holidays just for *qualifying* for the tournament—Trinidad and Tobago, the final team to qualify for the 2006 Cup, started partying on November 16, 2005, and arguably haven't stopped yet. Sure, the NFL claims the Super Bowl will get a brawny 350 million TV viewers worldwide, but that's peanuts compared to the Cup. The *draw* for the first round of the Cup got that. Can you imagine 350 million people tuning in to watch a bunch of paunchy men pulling pieces of paper out of bowls? Yet, somehow, they do.

Going into 2006, FIFA estimated that over half the planet would watch the World Cup finals; sociologists put the number closer to three-fourths. Virtually every television on the planet, at some point during the six-week finals, would display a World Cup match.

Having split time between the United States, Scotland, and Europe since childhood, I take this all for granted. But covering the World Cup is a weird proposition if you're based in America. Many Americans think the rest of the world is a little nuts for adoring a sport in which you can't use your hands and many games end in ties. American editors, then, have a passive-aggressive relationship with soccer* in general and the World Cup in particular. It kills them to spend money to send their reporters places for a sport they hate; on the other hand, they know enough people love it that they feel they'd better do something to cover it, even if it's in a half-assed way. It should go without saying that, as a result, most coverage of the sport in the United States is half-assed.

In 2002 the USA would unexpectedly reach the quarter-finals. (It should have reached the semifinals—this young American team outplayed the Germans, but made the fatal mistake of failing to score. After the match, the German coach, Rudi Völler, appeared before his nation's press, a pale, sweating, and shaken man. His first comment was that his team hadn't deserved to win.) The USA—a perennial also-ran in the sport—overnight was considered a world-class team. Americans woke up not only to the news that the USA was playing soccer but that it was *damn good* at it.

But, of course, the winter before the tournament, no one knew this would happen. All we knew then was that the World Cup was to be cohosted—for the first time ever—between Japan and South Korea. It was widely believed that the South Korean government had horned in on the deal, and there were whispers that politicians, in a departure from the standard,

---

Soccer and *football* are interchangeable terms for the sport of association football. Despite what some people think, the term *soccer*—which is popular in North America, Asia, and some other parts of the world—was coined about the same time as *football* was, and it was used to distinguish the sport from rugby, or *rugger*. The reason *soccer* gained such a foothold in America is easy to understand: It was to distinguish the sport from American football. In this book, we'll use the terms interchangeably, calling the sport *soccer* when dealing with the American team, and using *football* when we're talking about the rest of the world.

smoother forms of persuasion (i.e., flying in delegates, wining, dining, and gifting them, etc.), had outright bribed folks. Whatever they did worked: FIFA split the Cup between Japan and South Korea, making a lot of people's lives miserable.

The problem was, it was a ludicrous decision. Not only are South Korea and Japan separated by a large body of water, the two nations despise each other. South Korea was occupied by Japan from 1910 to 1945, and hatred of their historic oppressors occupies a big chunk of the South Korean consciousness.

(One thing you should never, ever do if you are running late in South Korea is ask a citizen about this period in the nation's history, as you will invariably be treated to an hour-long monologue on their neighbors and the terrifying nature of Japanese torture methods. People with strong stomachs are invited to visit the Seodaemun Prison History Hall in Seoul, which is a remarkably chilling exhibit of the various horrors the Japanese inflicted upon the Koreans.)

For Americans, the split location created a fiscal nightmare. With the economy in recession post-9/11 and newspapers firing folks left and right, the idea of a tournament that spanned two countries, involved a huge travel budget, and was in a time zone that meant matches in Asia would show live on U.S. TV at two A.M. drove my bosses nuts.

The Cup was also viewed as a dud of an assignment in the status-obsessed halls of journalism. Previously, the Cup was held in nice places such as Paris, Italy, or Argentina, and was seen as a plum junket for reporters of a certain age and stature in the sports department. Not this baby: *No one* wanted to go to South Korea, and my colleagues began to do elaborate things to duck the duty.

At one major East Coast metro paper, a prominent reporter I know showed up, in his words, "rip-roaring drunk" to the editorial meeting for summer coverage, hoping he'd be fired and thus avoid South Korea. Another told me he showed up in women's clothing. Others took vacation time. Some didn't show up at the office for weeks and stopped returning calls. Nothing worked: We went, albeit by force.

To be frank, I didn't know what to expect. I knew nothing about South Korea. I did know, however, that my well-heeled European friends were exploiting their newspapers' expense accounts in Tokyo and sending e-mails about the quality (and the gleefully horrifying costs) of food, hotels, and women. Envious, I felt that I was a bit hard done by.

I would be proved wrong. The 2002 World Cup ended up being not only one of the best World Cups ever held, but one of the most rewarding.

South Korea, I discovered in short order, is a spectacularly weird place that up until the World Cup was also quite sheltered from the rest of the world.

Because of its location, a wide peninsula that juts out from the bottom of China into the Sea of Japan, and its lack of exports, until the 1990s Korea was best known in the West as the site of a brutal, stalemated war. With the explosion of computer technology, however, South Korea underwent a startling transformation, going from a largely agrarian country to a semiconductor-driven powerhouse in the space of ten or fifteen years. Today South Korea is a reliable manufacturer of the cheap and disposable tech goods Wal-Mart has made its stock and trade in.

Despite the success of Daewoo and Hyundai, however, the South Korean people saw little of the Western world beyond the reach of their satellite dishes. This is perhaps unsurprising, considering that the country is still formally at war with its neighbor to the north and still houses an American military presence.

At the time of the World Cup, the South Korean government—led by a "reform" candidate who was pursuing what turned out to be an ill-fated "sunshine policy" with the North—wanted to show off its transformed nation and the Cup seemed like just the ticket. Tourists, at least ones without assault rifles, were expected to visit an industrious, cosmopolitan capital. Visitors to the southern coast, which does have some marvelous island and beachfront land, would be enchanted. South Korea would finally take its place as a leading nation.

Unfortunately, this was absurd. South Korea is crowded and incredibly polluted. The weather is nasty, like putting on a cable-knit sweater after a hot shower in the middle of July. Smog sits on the roadways, which are chaotic, crowded, and swift. The main highway—ten-lane, and built just for the Cup—runs tight alongside rice paddies, irrigating them in a stew of exhaust and gasoline. In the nearly two months I was in South Korea, I don't recall seeing the sun or the stars or the open sky once inside any of the cities.

South Korea's cities are also remarkably ugly. There are no houses. People live in large apartment complexes or in split-levels or above their shops. Seoul does have some green spaces—largely around temples, shrines, and royal buildings—but most of it looks like a decaying socialist city that was suddenly gussied up with a bit of neon.

This is perhaps best evinced in the building sited next to the main media center. It is one of those concrete boxes with an overhang and columns but with the unexpected flourish of a dome on top. It is incredibly ugly. I began to think of it as the "Central Reprogramming Center," as each morning there were people neatly queued up to go in; they left each night in the same neat lines.

What with the gray buildings, gray sky, gray air, and gray days, this doesn't sound like much fun at all, does it? Hardly a prime getaway, unless perhaps you're on vacation from Baghdad.

How the heck do the South Koreans deal with this? Well, they seem to be drunk a lot of the time. South Koreans drink spectacular, heroic amounts of alcohol. At all hours. All day long. It is culturally accepted that if you are a male office worker in Seoul, your idea of a nice night out with the boys starts with foaming pitchers of beer ingeniously cooled with dry ice, and *anju* (the bartenders look at you funny if you don't order any), then swiftly moves on to tumblers of scotch. The next step, or the "singing" phase, involves karaoke and carafes of whiskey. After that comes more *anju*. Then you repeat.

As you might imagine, there are an awful lot of taxis in Seoul that subsist entirely on carrying passed-out businessmen from bar to bar. Just because your head is on the table doesn't mean the night is over. Westerners are especially lucky: Their South Korean counterparts view them as ideal drinking partners. There were certain members of the British press corps who left for the first game, bright, chipper and neatly pressed, and never made it past the first bar, about sixty feet away from the press center. One fellow was still there on Day 15, unshaven, unkempt, unknowing, with the pallor of an eighty-proof diet.

Your average, run-of-the-mill night out, as far as I can tell, consists of all of the above with the addition of women and children. One curiosity of being in South Korea was that I never knew quite what time it was because families were up and out until all hours. Midnight? Just getting started!

No matter what their blood-alcohol saturation was, however, the Korean people were aggressively polite. People would actually get into rows over which fine citizen of Seoul got the privilege of taking you home to the wife and kids and stuffing you full of noodles and kimchi.

One night, early in my trip, I got caught in a downpour heading back to my hotel and was shocked when a young woman pulled her car up next to me, opened the door, and silently handed me her umbrella. I continued to see her each of the next few nights and began to think I was being stalked when I found out, quite by accident, that she worked for the Korean World Cup Organizing Committee and had been assigned to look after me. Somehow, that made things creepier.

My hotel was also a bit seedy. As near as I can figure out, most hotels in South Korea prior to 2002 existed primarily to facilitate prostitution. South Korea's government briskly cleaned up many of its "love hotels" on the eve of the World Cup, giving them at least a cursory face-lift. However, in the grittier areas of the country, the influx of Western journalists didn't seem a profitable—or expedient—replacement for the sweaty, loose-necktie, 20,000-won-an-hour businessmen the hotel staffers were used to. Not only did we talk funny, we made demands for odd things such as phone lines, lights, and hot water. As a result this new, alien system of hoteliering collapsed everywhere after about one week (even more swiftly in the case of a remarkably seedy subset of tabloid British journalists) and, at my hotel in Seoul, the owners started up the discotheques quickly once they figured out we weren't leaving.

In fact, prostitution seemed to be everywhere in Korea. Bizarrely, it was largely run out of barbershops. If you saw a single barber pole, you could get a haircut for 5,000 won ($3.50) and an ordinary Swedish-style massage for about 20,000 won. If you saw two barber poles, you could still get your haircut for 5,000 won, but massages cost about 80,000 for fifteen minutes of more personal service. And these barbershops were everywhere—fifteen of them ringed the COEX Press Center alone.

This created some havoc during the Cup. The Host Broadcast Services (HBS) staffers got a per diem of roughly 90,000 won a day—which they promptly spent at the barbershops. The media began to complain about this. They wanted a per diem of 90,000 won a day for the barbershops but, more important, the HBS staffers were stealing all the food meant for the press because they had no per diem left to buy their own.

While this was going on, one of the more intrepid broadcast women I met decided to get in on the action and went to several parlors where she and her pals were turned away. I gather at one point one of the women, a blond who stood about six foot one and looked as if she had a handsome low postgame, got irate about the lack of equal opportunity and caused a scene that reverberated all the way up to the Korean World Cup Organizing Committee. From that day on the edict was: no more per diems to be spent at barbershops.

This move was not well met by the owners and workers of said barbershops, who started grousing to the papers that the World Cup meant a lot of money and they wanted some, too. And besides, if they didn't get the money, they had all these videotapes of the clients.

The solution was genius: *Everyone* got a per diem and a box lunch. If only Congress were so wise.

I ran into my blond friend a day or two later and asked how things were going.

"They need work," she told me. "But they're getting the hang of it."

The games hadn't even kicked off and already I was damn sure this World Cup was going to be very, *very* different.

Hardest hit by South Korea were the Europeans, who left with some severely bruised egos. For once, this wasn't a World Cup held by the Europeans for the Europeans to win, and, sensing this, they began to panic once they hit the ground. They had good reason: Forced to play matches on truly neutral ground for the first time in a generation, they found the going heavy. Without their imposing stadiums and fans behind them, quite a number of European teams were revealed as very average.

First to go were the defending champions, France, who collapsed in spectacular fashion. Led in 1998 by their charismatic midfield engineer, Zinedine Zidane, the French epitomized beautiful soccer—they were marvels at one-touch passing, and looked positively symphonic when on the attack. In 2002, however, the French team arrived exhausted and beat up after a rough year in their leagues. Zidane, from top Spanish club Real Madrid, was hurt, and was tragically ineffective at orchestrating the French offense. The French striker, Thierry Henry—arguably the greatest forward in the game—had also had a grueling year at Arsenal, where his team had deservedly won both the Premiership and the F.A. Cup, and arrived in a fugue state.

The French would go on to do something no defending champ had ever done: go out after the first round. Their elimination in Incheon by Denmark, 2–0, was made even more surreal by the setting. The South Koreans had trained an enormous number of their citizens to do uncharacteristic things—whole armies of "home supporters" were bused in to cheer for teams they knew nothing about to make sides such as Mexico and France (neither of which had a large traveling fan contingent) feel more at home. This actually had the opposite effect: It was utterly disorienting. At the time, South Koreans knew very little about soccer, so they would cheer for things you wouldn't normally, such as throw-ins. Several players on the French team stopped cold during the match to look around in puzzlement.

Afterward, surrounded by eager South Korean reporters and a rabid French press corps, the French players were despondent. Zidane was almost in tears. What the French had called the "culture of victory" had been destroyed. To this day, it has not recovered. As the South Korean press asked their characteristically bizarre questions—they had blanket twenty-four-hour coverage about a sport they knew nothing about, after all—the faces of the French players grew longer and grimmer. They were in a hellish Wonderland, being asked about noodles, tracksuits, and cell phones after their biggest personal failure.

The teams weren't the only ones. Any Westerner was fair game for this curious citizenry. As I was returning from the Tek Center on the subway one day, a gaggle of young Korean women—there seemed to be very few men in public during the daytime—walked up to me and handed me a cell phone. All of them were either very tall or quite short. There were no "average"-size South Korean women as far as I could tell.

The voice on the other end said "Hello."

I said "Hello" back.

One of the girls took the cell phone from me, listened, then smiled and said something in Korean. Then she gave me back the phone.

I said "Hello" again. All I could think about was that I was a good 450 feet underground and this cell phone had great reception. I really wanted one.

"The girl asks you how you like Korea," said the operator, and I, slow on the uptake, got it: This was a translation service. I said I liked Korea very much. "What about Korea do you like?" Well, I said, I liked the food, and the people, and I liked the city.

This went on for about half an hour. Each girl took turns asking questions into the phone, then handing the phone to me or my neighbor, and one of us would reply. Then we'd start all over again.

Things all South Korean women apparently want to know from young American men:

1) "Do you like Korea?"

2) "Do you think Korea is a good team?"

3) "Do you use spoons?"

4) "Do people in America dance? Do they like gum?"

5) "Can we discuss shampoo?"

6) "How is my English?"

Just think what kinds of questions their press asked.

The French were by no means the only Europeans to fail. Mighty Portugal was stunned, losing its opening game to the USA 3–2. To this day, tapes of the Americans running right at the Portuguese, dismantling them with two quick first-half goals from John O'Brien and Brian McBride and a dreadful own goal* created by the precocious Landon Donovan, are watched by coaches around the world. It wasn't well known at the time, but the USA had had a secret weapon.

"It was the most heartbreaking thing I have ever done," Danny Gaspar told me over lunch one day after the Cup was long over. Gaspar, an internationally known goalkeeping coach of Portuguese descent with stints at Benfica, Nagoya Grampus Eight of Japan, and Sporting Lisbon, had been called by manager Bruce Arena before the Cup started, partly on my recommendation. "I told the U.S. coaches that Portugal couldn't handle it if you came at them," he said. "I was so torn, I couldn't watch the game. It was like seeing your parents argue."

Italy distinguished itself with world-class petulance. Its exit at the hands of the South Koreans became a nightmare for Ecuadorean referee Byron Moreno, who endured a campaign of character assassination after the fateful match. The Ecuadorean never recovered and quit the game a year later. "I prefer to die standing up than to live kneeling down," said Moreno on his way out.

South Korean Ahn Jung-Hwan, who scored the winning goal in that match, also paid a price: He was sacked by his Italian club, Perugia, the next day. Perugia's president, Luciano Gaucci, branded him a "traitor" and refused to pay him a salary any longer.

And then there was the press. Sergio di Cesare, head international writer for *La Gazzetta dello Sport*, was but one of

---

Own goal is a term used to describe a goal scored by a player into his own net. It's rather shameful.

many Italian journalists who tried to explain away his country's failure. "This result meant that the World Cup is now just a minor tournament for smaller nations," said Cesare. "Italy is happy to go home. They don't want to be there."

Sure.

The best was yet to come. In a tense, unbelievable quarterfinal, South Korea eliminated European soccer giant Spain on penalties. It was a controversial result: Spain had two goals waved off by the referee, Gamal Al-Ghandour of Egypt, and one of those was inarguably a legal and good goal. Spain should have won, but South Korea hung tough through 120 minutes of play and extra time to take the game to kicks. There, Joaquin made a critical miss from the spot, giving Korean captain Hong Myung-Bo a chance to win. He sunk the kick, and the nation partied anew.

"The truth was that the Europeans were arrogant," Eoghan Sweeney, the chief football writer for the *Korea Times,* said to me at the time. "They paid no attention to the emerging nations and it served them right."

But there was another story going on here as well. The lengths the South Koreans went to make visitors feel at home—even though the South Koreans clearly didn't understand anything about Western customs and most often failed spectacularly at aping them—had an unintentional side effect.

One night I went out for dinner with a young South Korean woman from the COEX. She took me to a district I had never heard of or seen on the map, filled with arcades, computers, and sushi shops. Here were all the young men—apparently their girlfriends gathered around while they played elaborate video games and then bragged about their prowess. She told me she would never be forgiven by her family if anyone thought we were on a date; her mother had already arranged a marriage to another office-dwelling South Korean man.

I asked her how often she had seen him.

"Twice."

This culture—with lonely men spending days in offices, bars, and video arcades, and lonely women left waiting for attention—was one of the major reasons World Cup games were almost overwhelmingly attended by young women.

Soccer in so many other countries is really often an excuse for men to get away from women for a little bit; in South Korea, with that dynamic turned on its head, the results were ones the government had not predicted. South Korea would go on to lose to Germany in the semifinals, and finish fourth after a loss to Turkey in the third-place match. But that was enough: The Korean team had done better than Japan and made an impression on their culture that lasts today. As the World Cup unspooled, women discovered the freedom that comes with being in a crowded stand. The World Cup "freed mature women and their daughters," according to University of Seoul professor Choi Yearn-hong, writing on July 1, 2002, in the *Korea Times*. The tournament "emptied the loneliness of apartments."

A taste of freedom can be a dangerous thing.

In the wake of the tournament, a new police chief would be elected—a woman who promptly cleaned up and unionized the city's vast prostitution trade. In a nation built on centuries of submission by women, women started to challenge their traditional roles.

I remained in touch via e-mail with a handful of young English-speaking women I met during the tournament. Since then, my "date" bowed out of her arranged marriage and has risen to a cushy executive position at a South Korea–based outpost of an American technology company. Another decided, to her mother's dismay, to leave South Korea and travel to Canada to learn about the outside world. A third one started a punk rock band. All of them still follow Korean soccer fervently, to the point that they now do what was once unthinkable—they criticize the men playing and coaching the sport.

South Korea qualified for the 2006 World Cup in Germany but to the nation's dismay looked shaky. One of my friends wrote me to say she hoped the coach would be sacked and another foreigner hired.

After all, in her words: "What do Korean men know about soccer? Not much."

So, come 2005, I had high hopes for Germany. I don't particularly like Germany, but after my bizarre experience in South Korea (and I'm not even going to start on the wooden penises for sale on the streets) I thought the Cup's return to Europe might be just as dizzying. I was heartened when enterprising Berliners opened a huge brothel next to their Nazi-era Olympic Stadium; cheered when Ghana made the grade, knowing full-well that the team traveled with a large contingent of witch doctors; and was positively overjoyed when the Australians made it in on the last day. They're nuts.

In December 2005, I left cold and damp Chicago to travel to the old East Germany for the first major event of the 2006 World Cup, the "draw." And it is here, as they say, that our story begins.

1

WINTER IN GERMANY

While junkets like the draw seem exciting to fans and out-siders—*You're going to Germany! How thrilling!*—the truth is that this part of the World Cup, however important for the teams and the competition, basically entails sitting in a mod-ified hall with a bunch of tables and computer hookups, star-ing at a large TV screen. In Leipzig, the draw was held like a trade show at a new convention center, essentially a long glass aircraft hangar, full of dour, chain-smoking Europeans des-perate to return to the hallway for another cigarette. The cen-ter's entrance was decorated with a steel rose by a Berlin artist. Viewed dead on, the sculpture looked like a thin, flaccid penis atop a set of glass balls—not the best omen. As the drizzle came on and the temperature dropped, the setting seemed in-creasingly depressing.

In times past, the draw had been a bit more convivial—a great time to meet colleagues, trade war stories, discuss the finer points of padding one's expense account, and, above all, get five interrupted minutes with a coach or VIP that went be-yond your standard, stage-managed interview session. How-ever, this draw set a new low in entertainment value. While the

German journalists seemed quite well taken care of, especially in the drinks-and-smokes department, by and large the rest of the Fourth Estate was seen as a necessary nuisance. The VIPs and their hangers-on snuggled and chatted in an entirely different building, carefully segregated from any journalists who might ask an unscripted question. FIFA did present some of the bigwigs for Q&A sessions . . . with the caveat that journalists couldn't ask anything. Instead, FIFA "media officers" would pose three questions to the VIPs, and the crowd would have the joy of dutifully recording their responses. Some of these "questions" bordered on the absurd, and others were declarative statements that wouldn't have been out of place in Pyongyang.

All this control freakishness was finally undermined by the bizarre events at the draw ceremony itself. While the world waited for the crucial groupings, we watched magician Hans Klok. This blond, white-shirted Aryan did a routine with the aid of several gamines.* The one clad in a bikini top and tights (who, along with "The Bod," did not pass muster with Iranian TV censors) didn't raise eyebrows among the jaded press corps. No, it was the one clad in full-on bondage gear and wielding a riding crop, who stuffed Klok into a steel box, that provoked nervous laughter. I'm still not sure if this send-up of the Nazi S&M stereotype was an example of Dutch humor or a case of slumbering organizers, but most watching in Leipzig sat stunned through the rest of the program. (The English tourist bureau, recognizing that such stereotypes are common, released an unintentionally funny

---

*Klok is actually Dutch, but most watching didn't know that. You can see pictures of this event at his Web site, should you wish: http://www.stage-touring.com/hansklok.

guide for English fans* that pleaded with them not to sing some of the more inflammatory terrace tunes . . . such as the evergreen "Ten German Bombers.")

By now you may well be asking, What is this "draw" thing, anyway? In a nutshell, the draw is a big ceremony where the nations that have qualified for the tournament learn their group seedings. It's the beginning of the World Cup finals, and the end of the qualification phase. The fact is, the World Cup is not a one-off event, but the end point of a four-year continuum.

Once a World Cup host is selected—usually six years before the Cup in question, to give the hosts time to prepare and to observe a tournament—a marathon starts. The qualification process, 210[†] nations chasing thirty-two slots for the next World Cup, begins almost as soon as the last one ends. For two years, nations play one another in a variety of competitions, because each region chooses its own qualifying format and schedule.

As a result, the qualifying process varies dramatically—CONMEBOL (Confederación Sudaméricana de Fútbol, or the South American Football Association) has been criticized for what is seen as a punishingly long qualification process. The smaller nations, the Mauritiuses, Vanuatus, et al., of the globe, start immediately in round-robin or knockout play to winnow the field, while CONCACAF (the Confederation of North, Central American, and Caribbean Association Football) has often

---

*The publication is called *Do's and Don'ts: A Guide to Avoiding Penalties.*
[†]Gibraltar, a contested bit of rock that's a British overseas territory as well as claimed by Spain, has been granted provisional membership in UEFA, setting the groundwork for it to enter a team. In 2006, however, only 209 nations were eligible.

used different regional competitions to decide automatic placements in its later qualification rounds. This time, it added an extra round, meaning the teams who reached Germany had to play eighteen games—as many as the oft-criticized CONMEBOL.

Each region is allocated a certain number of slots as well, adjusted after each World Cup depending on a region's representatives' performance in the tournament. CONCACAF sent four nations to the 2006 edition—Mexico, the USA, Costa Rica, and Trinidad and Tobago. Strong UEFA (Union of European Football Associations), on the other hand, sent fourteen teams.

Because of the tournament's size, the World Cup is broken into two stages. First is the group stage, where the thirty-two teams are placed into eight groups of four. Between the first and third weeks of June, these teams play each of their groupmates once. A team earns three points for a win, one for a draw, and nothing for a loss. Realistically, a country has to win at least one and draw one of the three first-round games (for four points) to have a shot at making the next round. A knockout round follows, winnowing the field to eight, and then it's quarters, semis, and the final. This all takes course over a thirty-day span, making the Cup a test of a team's endurance as well as its skill, to say nothing of the stamina of the reporters and the fans.

Some groups are tougher than others, making the draw quite important. In 2006 the group the USA was seeded into was one of the toughest—a *"grupo del morte"* in soccer parlance—with the Yanks having to face Italy, Ghana, and the Czech Republic. Reigning champions Brazil got a comparatively soft draw against Croatia, Australia, and Japan.

As only the two top teams in each group progress to the

knockout stages, a "good" draw is considered a favorable omen. What constitutes a good draw is debatable, however. Japan, for example, probably wasn't pleased that it had to play regional rival Australia, world champ Brazil, and a decent European side in Croatia. In fact, that draw pretty much spelled doom for Japan right from the get-go. On the other hand, the Aussies, who are gleefully crazy, cheered—loudly, heartily, drunkenly—at news of their selection in Brazil's group, shocking the hell out of the draw's presenter, the leggy German model Heidi Klum. With typical down-under panache, the Australians wanted to have a go at the world's top side, Brazil, partly because the Aussies are fearless, and partly because their kit (outfit) is based on that of the golden boys.*

During the group stage, when all the minnows are still in play, the twelve host cities are filled with each team's eager, hopeful cheering sections; the draw thus lets those fans know where to book their rooms. This might seem a throwaway point, but not nearly enough rooms are ever available for rent and those rooms rise exponentially in price as the tournament grows nearer. (Germany had to crack down quite a bit

---

*Weird trivia: Australia is one of just four teams at the top level that do not wear a kit based on the colors of its country's flag. The others are Japan (blue), Italy (also blue), and Holland (orange). Legend has it that the Socceroos (yes, that's really what the team is called) just started playing in the first kits they could get their hands on, and they were Brazilian copies. This isn't unusual. If you've ever wondered why (for example) Newcastle United of England and Juventus of Turin wear the same kit, it's because Juventus's owners liked the English kit, and replaced their team's rather sickly pink outfits with copies they'd brought home with them from Northern England. This was a bold, sensible move. On the same topic, if you've ever wondered why the USA didn't wear red on the field for a fairly significant length of time, it was because the ex-president of U.S. Soccer, Werner Fricker, thought red was "commie." Seriously.

on reported price gouging several months before the Cup started, but in the end, the market was said to be fair. Now, Japan for the 2002 World Cup—that was another story.) This alone makes the draw the unofficial financial beginning of the World Cup finals.

And as the Germans were intent on making this Cup the biggest sales event the planet had ever seen, with Germany itself the biggest and most expensive item on display, the choice of Leipzig to stage their first major public event as the Cup's hosts was hardly coincidental.

For some seven hundred years this unassuming Saxon city, best known to the outside world as the home of both Bach and Wagner, has been a center of world commerce, holding a twice-yearly showcase for commercial goods. This fair has run uninterrupted by famine, flood, or war since the Middle Ages. It was the world's biggest commercial sales event in the 1930s, and the city managed it with the help of what was, at that time, the planet's largest railway station.*

Arguably, without Leipzig, neither the World Cup nor the American companies that underwrite it would enjoy their present prominence, for American brands such as Gillette, Coca-Cola, and GM (all major soccer sponsors) honed their mass-marketing campaigns, and succeeded in cracking what had been a closed market, via the Leipzig fairs of the 1930s. With the money these American multinationals made in Leipzig, they built plants across the continent to serve a new group of consumers and lay the foundations of what would become

---

*See Victoria de Grazia's *Irresistible Empire* (Belknap/Harvard, 2005), p. 185. One small aside: de Grazia makes a number of strange claims in the midst of some otherwise interesting research, such as that Coca-Cola "invented thirst" to market its product inside Europe. Take that with a grain of salt.

a global marketing empire. Without Leipzig, which blossomed as a world-caliber market between the Weimar Republic and the Nazi regime, American companies would probably not have been secure enough in Europe to withstand the disruptions of World War II. For soccer, this American success proved to be fortuitous. Beginning in the postwar years, American companies, inspired by the phenomenal recovery the European economy experienced, embarked on an ambitious program to expand their market share across Europe and introduce American-style brand recognition. What better medium than the world's most popular sport? Since the late 1970s, American companies have been the main underwriters of the global soccer game, with Budweiser, Coca-Cola, MasterCard (and even Marlboro cigarettes!) providing the dollars to stage increasingly lavish productions. Though it's a safe bet that 99 percent of Bud drinkers in America wouldn't miss the sport if it disappeared overnight, Budweiser wouldn't be a global brand.

This so-called Americanization of Europe, and the impact consumerism has had on the continent's psyche, has been debated exhaustively by intellectuals on both sides of the political divide.* However, without these major companies— and the global companies that followed the American example (such as World Cup sponsors Yahoo!, Hyundai, Emirates Airlines, and T-Mobile)—the Cup would not be the massively rich tournament it is today. The 2006 edition of the Cup, with its overwhelming emphasis on tourism and mass marketing, would have had a very different face.

---

*For a more in-depth look at this phenomenon from a nonsoccer (and somewhat Marxist) perspective please see de Grazia's *Irresistible Empire* and John Brewer's intelligent dissection of the same in the *New York Review of Books,* LIII, no. 19 (November 30, 2006).

When the press corps had a minute, we set off for the sprawling Christmas Market (est. 1767) held during the draw. I spent five days gorging myself on the meats and pastries and spiked cider that were on sale from open-air carts placed about every ten feet. This is a street cuisine a guy could really get used to. In addition, the market sells locally made goods, everything from meats and cheeses to china and toys. I was amused that I could pick up a Yankees hat here to boot, a strange purchase under the famous bronze frieze of Lenin and workers that hangs on the edge of the Augustusplatz.

Leipzig itself is a showcase, still unspoiled by glass boxes and Bauhaus architecture. Even though I was hailing from house-proud Chicago, I spent an inordinate amount of time with my neck at a painful angle, balancing a cup of coffee in one hand and a notebook in the other. The biggest concentration of old buildings (as well as a ferocious number of Christmas-themed shops) is the Zentrum, the center city, which can occupy the sightseer for a day. It boasts Germany's only building on the list of world monuments, St. Thomas's Church. A marvel with a large white turret and accommodation for some 3,200 worshippers, it owes its greatest fame to having employed Johann Sebastian Bach as cantor during the early 1700s. For me, the long antiquarian district near St. Nicholas's Church—so many books and so much sausage—was so fascinating I unfortunately bumbled right into a middle-aged woman who did not feel this was "a time to make friends."*

Other Leipzigers probably had a bit more brio. I could have spent more time in the vibrant student/anarchist/"punk"

---

*The official FIFA World Cup 2006 slogan.

area along the Karl-Liebknecht Strasse on the south (sud) side of the city. Cafés and boutiques selling everything from purses to yarn line the strip for about ten blocks—think a sparser Greenwich Village. However, I was traveling with a fellow reporter whose sole mission was to find bratwurst. Several times, I tried to explain to him that bratwurst was not sold in this region of Germany, but to no avail. Every night, every few feet, he'd ask a perplexed resident where the BRAT-*vuuurst* was. He couldn't have sounded less like a grown man trying to speak German if he'd practiced. With each repetition, the volume increased, and the tenor of his voice grew to where he was channeling Dick Dastardly. This was both comical and embarrassing.

It also may have cursed him. He asked again at the all-meat, all the time Auerbachs Cellar, a setting for a scene in Goethe's masterwork *Faust*. Knowing a good thing, the modern cellar gamely plays off this heritage with an actor dressed as Mephistopholes who hops around the tables every night around ten. We didn't understand a thing he said to us, but it clearly had some effect, as one of the chairs collapsed, almost taking my sausage-soaked friend with it. He walked with a limp for the next few days.

Unfortunately, the question of darker history, and how to get away from it, remains in Leipzig today. Known as "Der Heldenstadt," or the City of Heroes, Leipzig was the crucible for the East German revolt against the Communist dictatorship; tens of thousands gathered here in a peaceful mass demonstration against the hated Stasi, or secret police, culminating in a bloodless coup. The former headquarters of the Stasi, on an otherwise placid street at the edge of the Zentrum, is now open to the public free of charge, and I made a stop there. Glorious outside, inside it is a large, dank building with nicotine-colored walls, ornate wood carvings, and heavy green industrial steel doors.

For nearly fifty years, men and women in suits sat here and judged their neighbors. Some of their pictures still hang in the offices; they are seen in parades, with chests so over-stocked with medals and ribbons it's a wonder they didn't topple over from the weight. There are ratty disguise kits, some the quality of which were sold to children in the back of comic books, others good enough for the stage today. There are far more sinister mechanisms displayed as well. Gas masks and radiation suits. Interrogation rooms filled with surgical gear. Phone taps. Cameras. Guns.

Surveillance photography is displayed throughout the building. It is banal and impenetrable. Pictures of men on the street, children in parks, women getting out of cars—out of context, it is the stuff of everyday life. Of course, that was what the Stasi sought to control.

When the revolution came, it came here first. The Stasi refused to open the doors, fearing they would be rent by the mob. Ultimately, they relented to a remarkably calm and peaceful group. They were no doubt surprised to find them-selves alive the next day—after all, that was a charity they never would have granted.

Today schoolchildren file in and out of the building with ease. When I left, a stern schoolmarm was trying to get her gaggle under control, to make them stop touching the wood-work, to behave, to stop being kids. One child traced the line of the lions' heads carved into the wall before she was called down the hall to join her group. Her shoes clacked as she pushed past another class that went laughing out into the rain.

2

WHY ARE WE HERE?

Welcome to Hamburg, the home base of Team USA. Finally we came to the week before the Cup—always the giddiest time for the fans and the people sent to work the games. Once the grind of the matches sets in, you tend to miss these first days when you have the luxury to sleep, bathe, and eat. It's a time of true silliness—the expectations of the matches are high, yet all the teams are sequestered, so folks like me go out in search of whatever can be passed off as news to the voracious editors back home.

Over the week we, and thus the public, would be treated to a variety of cheap, one-hit wonders. Some were genuine events set up by fans, others were attempts by admen to get face time for their products. There was the World Cup in Mud on the banks of the Elbe, which, disconcertingly, the island nation of Jamaica won; the World Cup of Ducks; the Penguin World Cup; and the FIFI World Cup of Tiny Nations, which included the breakaway nation of "St. Pauli," actually a region of Hamburg, Germany.

———

Home to the second-largest port in Europe, Hamburg boasts a notorious red-light district and a spiritual connection to the Beatles.* Little known to Americans today was the tremendous damage inflicted on the city during World War II, when the Allied firebombing campaign of 1943, Operation Gomorrah, literally turned the river to steam in an attack that leveled at least three-fourths of the city. Ordinary citizens were roasted alive in underground bunkers; those "lucky" enough to be outside were flayed by winds that reached 1,500°F.

Today Hamburg is best known in soccer circles for the fervent support afforded third-division St. Pauli, the rebels of the sports world. With the team playing in camouflage uniforms garnished with a pirate's skull and crossbones, the fans run the gamut from transvestites and communists to anarcho-syndicalist punks. St. Pauli, despite being awful on the field, is so popular it claims to sell the fifth-most merchandise of any club in the world, and the club is clearly admired by fans across the country.

Four days before the tournament opened, World Cup first-timers Trinidad and Tobago played a "friendly"† with FC St. Pauli at the club's Millerntor-Stadion, aptly located near the Reeperbahn. Tickets were impossible to come by: The 20,629-capacity ground had sold out weeks before, as the islanders' visit marked the second-biggest match of the year for

---

*The Beatles polished their sound in Hamburg bars from 1960 to 1962. Paul McCartney and then member Pete Best were actually deported from Germany in 1960 (after setting fire to a room) but the band returned to play in Hamburg in 1961, where the nascent group recorded a charting single as the backing band for Tony Sheridan. For more details on Hamburg and the influence it had on the Beatles' sound, see Astrid Kirchherr and Klaus Voormann's book, *Hamburg Days* (Genesis Publications, 1999).

†In soccer parlance, a "friendly" is an exhibition match.

the club, coming behind only the side's 3–0 loss to Bayern Munich in the semifinals of the league cup.

For one night St. Pauli supporters gave up their traditional black and white clothes for red T-shirts, provided by the T&T federation, that read SMALL COUNTRY, BIG DREAM. The Caribbean fans brought drummers and dancers, and the stadium became a giant festival. While the Soca Warriors defeated St. Pauli, 2–1, no one really cared about the result—the entire stadium cheered wildly for each goal. This little exhibition match really was one of the few that lived up to the Cup's aims of friendship and hospitality, and was a highlight of the Cup.

Across town, that same day, the USA played Angola in a closed-door match. The mood couldn't have been more different; the press was barred but reports leaked out that the game was rough, tense, and testy. This was in keeping with the atmosphere surrounding the American team, best described as a prison under deep lockdown.

How the heck did the USA get to the Cup in the first place? And how did it go from obscurity to popularity back home?

In the summer of 1989, the governors of American soccer were in big trouble. The North American Soccer League (NASL) was gone. Soccer limped on indoors with the Major Indoor Soccer League (MISL). The national team might as well not have existed. The last time the Americans had played in a World Cup was thirty-nine years before. And yet, somehow, FIFA had agreed to put its signature event in the United States in 1994. The world press was in an uproar—how could a country with no professional league, an amateurish national team, and no history of supporting soccer play host to the world's biggest sporting event? FIFA felt the heat; word leaked out that it had told the USA's organizing committee that if its national team could not make it through qualification for the 1990 World Cup in Italy, America would lose the right to host in 1994.*

The Hungarian-born Bob Gansler, who had toiled in the long-extinct National Professional Soccer League (NPSL) in the 1960s, was hired to coach the team and decided to take a team of amateurs pulled from the college ranks through qualification, leaving former NASL names such as Ricky Davis where they were, in the MISL. In the minute circle that was American soccer, this was a controversial decision, but Gansler paid the protests no mind.

Qualification proved to be tough; the United States dropped points at home with draws to Trinidad and Tobago and lowly El Salvador, and it went into its last game on November 19 needing a win in Port of Spain. It was an odd match: Observers noted that the Trinidadians seemed suspiciously sedate while the Americans played a frenzied, largely ineffective style. Late in the first half, Paul Caligiuri put one in the nets for the USA, scoring a goal the overeager American soccer press would dub the "Shot Heard Round the World." The Americans went to Italy, where they lost all three first-round games, but they did not humiliate themselves and the stage was set for 1994.

That particular year remains the most profitable World Cup of all time, and, here, the Americans turned to the Serbian manager Velibor "Bora" Milutinović, one of the most

---

*Those whispers were wrong, in fact: FIFA never put any explicit pressure on the USA ... but it was indeed implied. After the USA qualified for the Cup, however, FIFA did have a showdown with U.S. Soccer—over the man chosen to run it, Paul Stiehl.

colorful coaches in the sport. A carpetbagger of the first order, Bora (no one ever calls him anything else) is sly, manipulative, seductive, evasive, magical, frank, and opaque, all at the same time. I find him to be hilarious, but while there is a small, particular subset who find him charming, most people—including but not limited to anyone who has played under him—consider him a tremendous pain in the ass. The term most used to describe Bora is "Svengali," and that's about right.

Fun with Bora: The man speaks at least three languages fluently, yet enjoys pretending he has no idea what you're saying. In one encounter with the press, he explained to an American journalist asking a sticky question that "my English is not so good" before answering in fluent Spanish, which Bora well knew this particular hack didn't understand. He then defused an equally pesky Spanish-speaking member of the press by alleging that, well, his Spanish wasn't so good either, and so he'd have to answer in English. If he sniffed out the rare member of the American press who spoke more than one language, he'd switch to Serbian, or, in a pinch, answer with his favorite phrase: "I don't make comparations." This nonsensical response was trotted out whenever he was asked, well, about anything at all he didn't feel like "comparating."

Bora is also a world-class mooch; he makes a habit of showing up to games without credentials or tickets and always manages to smooth-talk his way in, often by attaching himself to a reporter who can vouch for his bona fides. I have had (repeated) personal experience with this. A classic Bora move came when he showed up at a match ticket window in Russia, sans wallet. He tipped down the tinted glasses he always wears, smiled slyly, and asked the ticket lady, "Do you know who I am?" Reader, he got in.

Bora's goal, wherever he coaches—and he's coached pretty much everywhere—is to make himself look like an amiable bumbler, just kind of getting by on his charm and politeness. This tactic conceals a mind brilliant and scheming, and not above the type of psychological manipulation that would make a Gitmo guard proud. With this MO, he typically enjoys about a year of grace before the people who employ him catch on that he doesn't take them nearly as seriously as they think he should. Usually this realization arrives at the onset of a major tournament, at which point he's got them over a barrel and can do whatever the hell he wants with their teams.

This may sound cavalier, but it must be said that Bora Milutinović fundamentally altered not only the American national team, but the entire world of soccer. In that respect, he's possibly one of the most important modern-day coaches, and despite his déclassé reputation (he'll never be asked to coach, say, Barcelona) there is no denying he can work magic with a very, very limited team. And, in 1993, that's exactly what he was handed.

What Bora figured out was this: The gap between the top six or seven teams in the world is fairly small; however, the gap between these seven teams and everyone else is pretty damn huge. To other people, this would be grounds for pessimism, but Bora shrewdly realized this meant a team ranked in the 60s by FIFA was probably not much worse than a team in the 20s. In fact, it might actually be easier to make a low-ranked team look better—just beat a few teams ranked higher than you (who really aren't that far above you in quality), and bingo: instant confidence. This was a true eureka moment in the game and it has had far-reaching implications; now, instead of trying to knock off the big guns, a number of teams cherry-pick matches against "better" teams who are over-ranked or in a slump. In other words, Bora realized that a loser has nothing to lose.

So, how do you level the playing field? Bora took one look at the players he had available to him and decided the first thing to do was to teach them how to foul. While this might run contrary to the "fair-play" notions of the game, fouling isn't always a bad thing. For one, if you foul intelligently, you can break up the flow of play and rattle an opponent; for another, every time you take the ball away and force your opponent to reset, time keeps running off the clock, bringing you that much closer to the game being over.

The second thing he did was disabuse the American players of any thoughts they might have harbored that they knew how to play the game. He told them bluntly that they didn't and used various exercises to humiliate any doubters.

The final thing he did was train the players to play one specific role, and that role alone. A classic example of this was Cobi Jones, a fleet winger who was prone to drifting inside. Once when play stopped during a friendly game, Bora stormed out of the coach's box, grabbed Jones's arm, and showed him exactly where he should be on the line.

All of this was wrapped in Bora's trademark persiflage and further complimented by his ambiguous and contradictory pronouncements to the press. A player who had a decent game was publicly savaged, while a guy who tripped over the ball as it was rolling at him could sometimes be praised. This left the players utterly confused about where they stood with him on the team and, in more than one case, near tears. While these tactics are widely in use in other American sports, they had never been seen in American soccer, which at the time was a white-collar, upper-middle-class, spoiled-kid sport.

Bora knew how to work the press, too. Unfailingly, he praised whatever team the USA played, selling the idea that opponents as disparate as Macedonia and Argentina were somehow equal. This worked because the press corps were largely local guys who had been chucked onto a beat they knew little to nothing about and were thus easily bamboozled by cryptic pronouncements. Bora's favorite line was, "You must know who you play," a phrase that reinforced insecurities in the largely uninformed media corps. And let's be honest: Every team was tough for the USA in those days.

As a result, Bora had to consider every possible angle. He knew the USA had already qualified for the World Cup as host, so his real intent was to get the team past the first round. All he had to do was get four points—a win, a draw, and a loss—as the Cup, with only twenty-four teams at this point, would take the four best third-place teams to the knockout round. All Bora had to do was finish *third*.

On the field, the most challenging part of his job was teaching the USA the fundamentals of the professional game: how to kill a game, how to run the trap, how not to lose. Games were nail-biters; the Americans could blow a game at any moment and were never out of the woods until the final whistle blew. Watching them was agonizing but thrilling at the same time. One minute, the USA looked like a real soccer team, passing, dribbling, shooting; the next, they looked as if they had never seen a soccer ball in their lives.

Each game brought new adventures. There were passes right to the other team's forwards, heroic goalkeeping displays that kept the USA hanging on by their collective fingernails, an inability to keep the ball inbounds for more than a minute or two. There were also dazzling bursts of speed and skill that were as unpredictable as the Santa Ana winds, and gritty performances from guys you felt sure were moments away from collapse. The team wasn't very good, but it had a lot of heart, and most of the players were nice, thoughtful guys to boot. It was hard not to root for them and get caught up in the action.

When the Cup opened that summer, everything went to plan. The USA drew with the Swiss, beat Colombia, and lost to Romania, to finish third in Group A; then went on to play a halfway decent game against eventual champion Brazil to exit the Cup.

Success.

Predictably, few in American soccer realized how much of this had been accomplished with smoke and mirrors, choosing instead to believe that the USA had finally "arrived." The honchos proclaimed it "time for an American coach" to help "sell the sport" for 1998, and Bora was sent packing (to rival Mexico, one of his many stops). The hopelessly out-of-his-depth Steve Sampson was given the job.

Sampson turned out to be the Gregor Samsa of American coaching: He woke up one day and, with no rhyme or reason, his life had utterly changed. And, like Samsa, he lost it.

I have some sympathy for Sampson, largely because it was pretty obvious the USA didn't have a lot of talent. He joined the team prior to 1994 as one of the assistants and his role was, in a nutshell, to pick up the cones after the guys were done practicing. He was jolly, he was nice, and he was clueless. It would transpire that he also lacked any sense of proportion when it came to team management. But on the plus side he was fluent in Spanish, so he could help "export" the American team to the country's own imported Latino population.

Sampson's ego ballooned to laughable proportions after his promotion and a few early wins in the 1995 Copa America. The team was loose, happy to be out from under Bora's relentless scrutiny, and Sampson mistook that pleasant atmosphere for expertise on his part. He started having grandiose "chats" with the media, holding forth on matters he clearly knew little about. He debuted a self-proclaimed "revolutionary" tactical system, the 5-4-1 formation* . . . which his players found incomprehensible. He was enamored with strange team-building exercises, such as a word of the day, that made him a figure of fun, not least among his team.

Unfortunately, the choices Sampson made were damning. A complicated man, Sampson grew up under a domineering father and his life would be marked by a need to please, combined with an extremely fragile ego. Once put under stress, Sampson became a powder keg just itching to blow. He took every bit of criticism personally and had a habit of calling reporters late at night to complain about their coverage of the team at a time the sport was literally begging papers and TV to come to the games. Team captain John Harkes, who could mimic Sampson with devastating effect, quickly figured out his coach's weaknesses and mocked him relentlessly behind his back. Sampson found out, and Harkes, once named

---

*Here, history may grant Sampson a reprieve. At the time, he was openly mocked for this, largely because of the pomposity with which he debuted the system. But guess what? A lot of teams today use a lone striker and a five back/midfielder combination. He might have been onto something.

"captain for life," was abruptly kicked off the team.* With this unpopular dismissal, deep fissures opened between the veteran core of players and the replacements, and between players and coach.

Sampson could also be breathtakingly ham-handed. In an attempt to prune the team of some deadwood, he imported David Regis, a Frenchman with a tenuous American connection, to provide cover at the back... and had him bunk with the player whose place he would be taking, Jeff Agoos. Agoos was so distraught he considered quitting soccer altogether, but because he cared about the U.S. team more than anything else, he said nothing and agreed to help acclimate the befuddled Regis. Regis spoke little to no English and couldn't figure out what the heck he'd gotten himself into, much less why everyone seemed to hate his guts.

Time wore on, the pressures built, and Sampson became so tightly wound that people began to worry about his health and sanity. The team was a wreck even before it stumbled into France for the 1998 World Cup, an unmitigated disaster for the USA. Team members were at one another's throats, and when the USA lost a critical second game to political rival Iran, Sampson melted down at the press conference. He was

---

*Harkes subsequently wrote a book about this, with Denise Kiernan, with the amusing title *Captain for Life and Other Temporary Assignments.* Interestingly, while Harkes's dismissal seemed abrupt to fans and most people in the outside world, insiders saw it as agonizingly drawn out. Why? Because Sampson had told people privately that Harkes would be removed as early as December 1997. So, when Sampson didn't lower the boom until the following spring, the effect of Harkes's ouster was that much rawer for the folks who had to run the team.

fired a few days after the final game against Yugoslavia and he isolated himself with his family in California. Bora was at that game, watching both of "his" teams.

When I last spoke with Sampson in person, over lunch in Korea, he recognized that he made certain roster moves too late, and he was honest about the tension and fissures on the team. But he seemed incapable of admitting or understanding his role. When he spoke about it, it was almost as if "Steve Sampson" hadn't been there at all—that person in France was someone else entirely. It was creepy, and I'm pretty sure at this remove that I left most of my lunch uneaten.

Sampson has been rehabilitated somewhat after a successful run as the first American to coach a national team outside the USA; the Spanish-speaker did a good job with the Costa Rican national team before falling victim to politics. In 2006 he was fired as coach of the Major League Soccer (MLS) team Los Angeles Galaxy after Alexi Lalas, one of his disgruntled former players, was hired as the GM.

After the disaster in France, U.S. Soccer was in disarray. Due mainly to the fact that six weeks in Paris was a nice junket for a press corps otherwise indifferent to the sport, the team's performance had not gone unnoticed. And the fact that political tensions were high between the United States and two of the nations whose teams had beat the Americans in the 1998 Cup—Iran and Yugoslavia—just magnified the woes heaped on the team, the coach, and anyone else associated with the sport.

After flirting with the Portuguese coach Carlos Queiroz, U.S. Soccer chose then D.C. United head coach Bruce Arena to take the helm. Arena, a former soccer and lacrosse player, had actually appeared once as goalkeeper for the national team (back when no one was paying any attention) but he was best known for the soccer program at the University of Virginia, which he turned into an NCAA powerhouse. Arena got lucky during his tenure: Claudio Reyna went to U.Va. on an academic scholarship and happened to try out for the team, changing both men's careers forever. But Arena produced a number of excellent players who also made their way into the pro ranks. After becoming head coach at D.C. in 1996, Arena soon made the young MLS team into a regional contender, winning the league title, the U.S. Open Cup, and the CONCACAF Champions Cup. There was little question he was the best American coach yet produced.

Better yet, on the surface, Arena was the polar opposite of both Sampson and Bora. He was fiercely protective of his team and adept at working with players of varying skill levels. Arena, more than any other American coach, also grasped the nuances of tactical play. Though in public he downplayed tactics, in private he and his coaching staff spent countless hours looking over videotape and plotting detailed attack plans against every opponent.

Arena, however, came with a big downside—his ego. Arena is a strange man; he's unquestionably bright and competent but also insecure and impatient. Often described as "abrasive," he has a disquieting habit of emotionally and verbally abusing people he finds mentally inferior to him. Where Bora defused idiocy in public with gentle humor, Arena publicly mocked silly questions and ignorant reporters. Paradoxically, he was honest, straightforward, and almost charming in a one-on-one situation. But when the klieg lights were on him, he could be insufferable, even cruel.*

That behavior immediately caused waves behind the scenes. Two cases in point: His media relations officer, Rich Schneider, quit because of the abuse Arena heaped on him and others; another staffer was fired and then rehired after it became abundantly clear she was the only one skilled enough to do her job. As his tenure went on, Arena became more and more grating to people inside and outside the team, prompting critics to wonder if his demeanor was hurting the sport's attempt to sell itself in the United States.

During games, Arena's behavior cost the USA. Sideline cameras often caught him making a scene; it went so far some enterprising soul made a compilation of Arena's tantrums to demonstrate how out of control he was. There is an unwritten rule in the sport that, no matter how much you disagree with a call, you don't attempt to humiliate the ref personally. A chronic whiner, Arena crossed that line so often refs began to pay the team back by ignoring fouls and not giving the USA the benefit of any doubt. But such shenanigans could be ignored as long as the USA won games.

With the Korea/Japan Cup in 2002, a neutral site helped an American team use stealth and preparation to overcome shortcomings in talent. But 2006 would be different. After a quarterfinals finish in 2002, everyone knew about the American players. And for once, so did American sports fans.

---

*For the record, I always got on with Arena just fine, but his treatment of other people at all levels was so public, blatant, and unfair that it was hard to respect him.

These folks don't watch many MLS games. They don't see college soccer games, unless they pass them clicking through the TV channels, looking for the Knicks. They might catch a few European games—maybe the Champions League final, or big games in England—but they're not the folks who show up at the pub at six A.M. religiously to catch Portsmouth-Everton in the dead of winter. They talk baseball; they know what's going on in the NFL; they can tell you how many triple-doubles Jason Kidd has put up in his career; they listen to sports talk radio and they follow their college teams avidly. What makes these folks different is that, for some reason, they've discovered international soccer and they like it. Maybe it was the Mia Hamm ad for Gatorade. Maybe they went with a pal to catch a game and got hooked. Or maybe they just happened to turn on the TV one day to discover that a game they thought was slow and boring was actually quick, passionate, and thrilling. These folks form the most important group of soccer fans in the States.

The so-called casual sports fans actually make up the most important group for *every* American sport; without them, no league or sport can really succeed. Why? Because there are a lot of them. These folks are the people who drive the ratings of baseball during the World Series. They turn the NBA from a little-watched TV sport into a big deal come the playoffs in June. And they make the Super Bowl the most-watched one-day sporting event in the world.

As it happens, American soccer has done a bad job of reaching out to them. MLS has spent time trying to convince the European and Hispanic fans to come see games; U.S. Soccer has spent an equal amount of energy trying to convince knowledgeable fans that its product matches up with the best in the world. The thing is, these casual sports fans don't really care all that much—they're the purest consumers of America's entertainment culture. They want to show up and see the big game and the big stars. In 1999, when the Women's World Cup became a summer smash, it was they who tuned in to Letterman, they who filled the Rose Bowl, and—by the same token—they who melted away after the Cup wrapped.

The key thing here is that these folks know sports. They've watched the big games, they remember how the USA has performed, and they were excited about the 2006 World Cup.

And guess what? These folks would be the American team's undoing.

All this time, something was missing for soccer in America, and that was attention. But since 1990, the U.S. national side had gone from an unknown, almost irrelevant team in a sport staffed by well-meaning volunteers to a quasi-professional concern that made millions, albeit still staffed by well-meaning volunteers. Some, like Alan Rothenberg, president of the U.S. Soccer Federation, realized the pitfalls inherent in this and tried to overhaul the Federation in the wake of the 1994 World Cup. They had only limited success, and as a result of the sport's continued amateurism, one of U.S. Soccer's biggest failures has been dealing with acceptance.

Fifteen years is a long time in the sports world—it took only a decade for horse racing to collapse as America's number-one draw, and hockey is now coming to terms with having gone from "can't miss" to "who cares" in just a five-year span. In fact, when change comes in sports it tends to happen quickly, as pro football found out in the 1960s. But the line between a fad and a sport with staying power is slim, and soccer's past incarnations have burned people. Yet, in 2006, something was fundamentally different, and this book is one of the many pieces of proof. If you had asked me what I thought the chances were for a full-length soccer book being published by a major house in America even four years ago, I would have laughed. Back then America's pro league was still considered shaky; today no one asks if (or when) MLS is going to close its doors. Five years ago, the Americans were not the unquestioned kings of their region; today, the USA is the team to beat in North America.

We're still dealing with forty-some years of psychological fallout, however. Soccer players are no different from any other athletes—they're confident, some even cocky—but they have come up through a system in which they're on the bottom of the pole in terms of respect and prestige. As a result, they're a little defensive about their sport, as if they'd spent a number of years being bullied by linebackers. The folks who market and run soccer games are worse: Some are downright paranoid in their insecurity. And the hard-core fans? Half of them wish everyone else would go away so they could get back to their Dungeons and Dragons–esque club, and the other half spends an inordinate amount of time driving editors crazy with ever more fanciful demands for coverage.

This has led to a bizarre situation where the sport is, on the one hand, desperate for people to come to games and talk about it and, on the other, deathly afraid of criticism and attention. This schizophrenia hit new highs in the run-up to 2006, when the players and team—for the first time—were treated like other pro sportsmen in America. Make no mistake—not one of the players on the American team was a legitimate international star. But some began to be treated and marketed as if they were.

There were Gatorade ads, Pepsi commercials, Letterman

appearances, conference calls. There were guest slots on MTV and major magazine features* and breathless interviews with scantily clad women of a type that surrounds each and every major sporting event. After years and years of begging editors at newspapers to, please, just put in the scores, suddenly the tables were turned. The reporters and the fans were here, knocking at the door.

Marcelo Balboa, a star defender on the 1990, 1994, and 1998 World Cup teams, was floored by the turnaround. Balboa, from my reckoning, inhabits a constant state of gentle amazement, not least for the reason that he went from no-nonsense defender to a lushly coiffed TV analyst. I once stood by him at an American team practice in Florida, and on that day he was amazed about his feet.

"When I was playing, I wore like a size nine," said Balboa, who seemed to be wiggling his toes inside his shoes. "I had no toenails 'cause they'd always fall off in my socks. Now I wear a nice size twelve. Look at my feet!" He looked right at me with a big grin, wiggling. "They're comfortable!"

ESPN hired Balboa to be the color man on the World Cup broadcasts, alongside new-to-soccer Dave O'Brien, whom the network had moved over from high-profile baseball coverage. ESPN thought O'Brien would lend the sport the necessary gravitas and credibility; previous U.S. national team games had been called by a series of guys who were, in all honesty, pretty much bottom tier.

Until 1994, Americans could see a lot of soccer but almost never the American national team. The soccer that

---

*By the way, this was great from a business standpoint for yours truly. I wouldn't want it to be thought I was looking a gift horse in the mouth.

Americans did see was imported, complete with top-tier production values. *Soccer Made in Germany* in the '70s had Toby Charles; Univision put on games with Andrés Cantor and Tony Tirado; and every British match was called by some of the best announcers in the sport.

After the 1994 World Cup, ESPN was forced to televise the games, which the network did in a grudging, erratic fashion because no one watched. As recently as 2002, the region's major tournament, the Gold Cup, wasn't broadcast in English. This created a situation whereby (a) Americans were familiar with (and spoiled by) top-class production values, and (b) the United States, on the other hand, didn't train any homegrown announcers. The Americans who did call games were not unlike the players; they had to train themselves, and they did it simply because they liked the sport, not because they thought they could make a living at it.

Today, soccer fans in America still get to hear international games called by the best announcers in the world; if you tune in to watch a Premiership game, you hear Martin Tyler on Fox or Setanta Sports because the game's feed is supplied, announcers and all, by British Sky Broadcasting (BSkyB). But there is no comparable top-quality feed for American games. Think about the result: How jarring would it be if you were watching an NBA game and suddenly Marv Albert was replaced by an amateur or a fan? You'd notice, right? So, when fans started tuning in to American games, they noticed damn quick what was missing. And they were upset.

Let's be fair here: When ESPN started broadcasting the U.S. national team games it lacked the viewership that might have spurred the network to start building up a bull pen of talent. Soccer was getting ratings so low that in some cases the final Nielsen ratings were in the statistical realm of error. As a result, when O'Brien and Balboa came on the scene, it was, in a sense, too late. The 2006 World Cup telecasts on ESPN were not well received, and O'Brien and Balboa in particular were panned. O'Brien was so hurt by some of the catcalls he considered quitting the gig after the Cup.

The more philosophical Balboa didn't seem concerned, declaring, "Hey, I had a great time!" Don't take this to mean Balboa was blissfully ignorant. He did notice, quite swiftly, that this was going to be a different World Cup.

"We had no clue what we were getting into in 1990," Balboa told me. "I'm not even sure we had any expectations. We were college kids, and we went, and a couple people knew we were there, but it happened and then we were home. The end.

"In 1998, again, no one really knew. It was a wonderful experience, but I don't think internally we ever thought we had a chance in France. There was so much turmoil that we never knew what the hell was going on. We were confused, and it showed on the field. And then stuff came out in the papers, with Coach and us firing back and forth . . . the team just combusted. But I don't even know if us players knew what to expect there, and, you know, we came home, and that was the end, too.

"But in 2006 there were *expectations*. We were being told that 'this was the deepest team ever' . . . At the very least, they had to get out of the first round."

From 1999 to 2004 the team performed well. Arena recognized the need for the program to be fully professionalized and pushed hard for improvements both in public and behind the scenes. He excoriated his old employers in the MLS for not producing enough top-level talent and individual teams for failing to make the players' everyday work environments challenging and meaningful. But he also rewarded those players who chose to stay and play in the United States, at times fielding national teams comprised entirely of MLS players, and he was applauded for it. None of us saw where this strategy would lead.

The first inklings of trouble came in March 2006. The USA traveled to Dortmund to face off against Germany in a friendly match that was vitally important for both teams. Germany needed a win: They had just been whipped 4–1 by Italy and an atmosphere of uncertainty swirled over the team. Coach Juergen Klinsmann was under heavy fire from all corners—to the point that the German legislature debated censuring him. German success in the Cup was a major issue and the infighting became so intense that then-new Chancellor Angela Merkel felt compelled to step in and defend Klinsmann in public.

"I can't say if the pressure [on Germany] will benefit us or not," Arena told reporters the day before the game. "In the big picture, however, a result is not that big of a deal for either team. I believe that's the same for each team. The result tomorrow is not as big a deal as it would be in the World Cup."

Arena, who always likes to take pressure off his side, was not being entirely truthful. The fact was that the game would have huge ramifications, and his players knew it. The USA has historically been snakebit in Europe, winning just a handful of friendly matches and never one with any real meaning. Earlier that month the USA had downed Poland 1–0, but the Dortmund game was far bigger, and the team hoped to show it could perform under the gun.

"There's been a bit of anxiety in camp this week," midfielder Pablo Mastroeni admitted before the game. "A lot of attention has been put on this game by the German press, so we're just at the point where we want to get things rolling. There is going to be a huge crowd and we're facing a very good team in a World Cup year."

This match also was held under somewhat odd circumstances. Because it did not fall on an official FIFA match day, clubs were not obligated to release their players to either team. As a result, the USA could not field a full-strength side. With the exception of two players from England's Reading, keeper Marcus Hahnemann and Bobby Convey, only players with MLS teams or those based in Germany got dispensation to play. Three key players were also out injured: Eddie Pope, Claudio Reyna, and Landon Donovan all watched from the sidelines.

But the USA was confident. Forward Taylor Twellman told reporters the team was ready: "They [Germany] are going to come flying at us," said Twellman. "But we're not here to get rolled over—we're here to get a result."

The first half of the game was a pretty even affair, right enough, and it looked as though it might be another long night for the German team, who left the field at halftime to boos from the crowd of seventy-six thousand. But in the second half the USA gave the ball away at the kickoff, forcing defender Steve Cherundolo to commit a hard foul to stop a German breakaway. On the ensuing free kick, Bastian Schweinsteiger lofted the ball into the box, where it bounced, untouched, into the back of the USA's net. Things got worse from there. The Americans ended up conceding three more goals and left Dortmund shell-shocked.

"Tonight was a reality check for us," said a seething Kasey Keller, the USA's goalie, after the game. "I don't think I can express how I feel in words you guys can print. I think some of us thought we could walk out on the field and kick the shit out of anyone. Maybe some of these guys took our [high] ranking too seriously."

Arena, who usually shouldered all blame, admitted that he wished he hadn't taken a "second-string team" to play Germany. "I think you saw that the MLS guys were very unfit to play at this level."

The Germans came away from the game reenergized, but the Americans were in no mood to be charitable. "Who cares about the Germans?" said Keller. "I care more about what this does for us. Maybe we needed our ass kicked."

Maybe, but the hangover from the Germany game seemed to last a long time. In May the Americans held a three-week-long camp in North Carolina and played a series of tune-up matches in the States. Players and observers alike told me the camp's atmosphere was tense. The European-based players and the MLS-based athletes separated into cliques; there was concern over a key member of the squad, DaMarcus Beasley, who was mired in a deep slump; and there were divisive questions over some players who had been omitted from the roster—and some who had been included.

One of those players was the mercurial John O'Brien, an undeniably talented player who helped steer the USA to great success in 2002 but has been dogged by injury ever since. O'Brien's career trajectory had taken a disturbing turn just prior to the World Cup: He had left Dutch giant Ajax for provincial ADO Den Haag, then suddenly signed for MLS's Chivas USA. At all three clubs, he had logged little playing time, and two senior staffers at ADO Den Haag told me the club's doctors could find little evidence of the injuries O'Brien claimed to be suffering. O'Brien came to camp out of form, and though his raw talent was never in question, there were a lot of raised eyebrows at his inclusion.

The team was now feeling a great deal of pressure, in part because it was being sold to sports fans as one of the best groups ever assembled by the USA. This weighed heavily on the shoulders of a number of players who had proved themselves in America but had never been under the world spotlight.

Finally, the USA had also booked a strange series of opponents for their warm-ups—Morocco, Venezuela, and Latvia—of whom only Morocco was of true international quality. Ostensibly, these sides were chosen because they played in fashions similar to those of the teams America would face in Germany, but it sure looked as though the USA was scraping the bottom of the barrel when it came to finding opponents.

The USA played Morocco first, meeting the North Africans in Nashville, and lost on a last-minute goal. It was an all-around disaster. Key defender Cory Gibbs was hurt and out for the entire World Cup. Claudio Reyna left the game hurt after only sixteen minutes. The USA didn't get a shot on net until the second half. Afterward, a chastened Arena told the press that the team was perhaps "a little overtrained," and the players agreed with him. Keller opined that the game "had knocked the team back a bit."

The USA next beat Venezuela and Latvia on its way to Germany, but hardly in convincing fashion. Yet, as the USA left for Hamburg, the PR machine was running at full power, with ESPN and ABC running spots touting the team and the networks' coverage, and major newspapers doing the kind of big takeouts that U.S. Soccer had never before received. Even sports talk radio* got into the act, and, to my knowledge, only one reporter† ventured that this team would be lucky to get out of the first round. That report was savaged in the fan blogosphere.

Expectations for this team were, in hindsight, stifling. Think about this for a minute: The USA, placed with a former World Cup champion, one of the best Central European sides, and an emerging African power in one of the Cup's toughest groups, was expected to not only survive but win. This view was delusional but widely held. For the first time ever, Team USA was under the kind of pressure soccer teams from around the world face on a weekly basis. The problem was that these guys—many of whom were deeply sheltered athletes—were not ready for the pressure cooker.

Other national teams had their own concerns. The Argentine delegation, uncertain that quality meat would await them, cunningly brought their own. They flew in almost four hundred pounds of beef for a barbecue. Pregame and postgame barbecues are a tradition for most Argentine clubs, which drives their nutritionists batty.

Meanwhile, in England, an entire nation waited by their radios and TV to find out whether Wayne Rooney, their exciting and arguably irreplaceable star, would take part in the Cup. Rooney had broken his foot in a league game and speculation over whether he'd be fit in time had pushed other news—politics, fuel, extraordinary renditions—off the front

---

*I know this from personal experience: WFAN, the New York agenda-setting station that normally never mentions the sport, called me in Germany to do a live spot at halftime of the USA-Ghana game.
†Go ahead and take a wild guess.

pages in the United Kingdom. Given the breathless tone the English brought to the matter, you'd have thought it was the hottest topic at the Cup. It wasn't.

Rooney's injury was part of a bigger discussion in world soccer, though. The World Cup is preceded by a congress of the FIFA Executive, and in 2006 the young English forward's name surely came up. That's because the big issue that year was compensation. Manchester United wasn't real keen on having Rooney suit up for England, because he was on Man U's payroll, not England's, so it would suffer any losses if he was injured. Rooney is a major financial asset, and his owners weren't happy to loan him out to folks who might play him against Paraguay with a less than fully healed foot.

Unlike the World Cup, which is a competition between nations—in other words, you have to be a citizen (technically, just a passport holder) of England to wear an England jersey or a citizen of Mali to wear the Malian strip—club soccer is league play, akin to America's NFL or NBA, with the caveat that every country has its own league. In England, the top division is known as the Premiership; in Italy it is called Calcio Serie A; in Spain La Liga; in Germany the Bundesliga; and so on around the planet. There are a number of lower leagues in each country as well, and a peculiar system of moving between them called promotion and relegation.*

---

*The easiest way to understand the concept is as follows: Say the Cleveland Browns have another awful season. Instead of playing next year in the NFL, they are forced (because they are so bad) to play in either NCAA D1 or the CFL (Canadian Football League). In turn, whichever team won the NCAA title or the Grey Cup gets to come up into the NFL. While this sounds rather cruel by American standards (and would give NFL owners apoplexy), this system has been in force in soccer all over the world for over a century.

The Champions League, organized by Europe's governing body, called UEFA, is a clever attempt to present the best club soccer from all across Europe in one place. So, at the beginning of each season—typically in August—the winners of the leagues across Europe are grouped together and play each other in a de facto "super league." Each year the Champions League final changes its host nation. The game serves as the unofficial end of the European season and the beginning of the summer "break." It's also one of the few European soccer "events" that cracks the cloistered world of American sports coverage. ESPN paid for and carries Champions League games live, and the final will make *SportsCenter,* the network's flagship program. The European Cup, once a somewhat down-market event, is today big business.

This worries the folks at FIFA, and with good reason: The truth is, soccer fans across the world get to see high-quality soccer all year long every year now and end up developing loyalties to club teams such as Manchester United or Barcelona rather than following their countries in the World Cup. This, of course, cuts FIFA out of the money chain and makes it very upset, because FIFA, if nothing else, is very good at acquiring and spending money, primarily on itself.

Today's crowded world soccer schedule also means that almost every top club now has to play for four major honors in a season:* the European Cup (or its sister tourney, the

---

*This means the clubs that lift titles are usually the ones that have had to make some painful choices along the way. Arsenal, for example, without ever overtly saying it, clearly played for *fourth* place in the English Premier League in 2005. It was a gamble, but a calculated one, based on the idea that if Arsenal could preserve its forces for the "big" Champions League games and still finish high enough in the table to gain a playoff berth for next season's

UEFA Cup), their own league's title, a league cup competition title, and the country's version of the "F.A. Cup," which is an in-country competition open to all teams that are members of the nation's Football Association. Perversely, all this hardware takes a bigger toll the better one's club is,* leaving the better players tired out before they even get to FIFA's World Cup.

In the larger scheme of things, issues like Rooney's foot are nudging the big European clubs toward doing what most observers feel would be in their best interest—breaking away entirely from FIFA, UEFA, et al., and forming their own "super league." You know, kind of like what those radicals at MLB and the NFL did.

To address the compensation problem, FIFA announced it was trying out a new form of insurance system, broadening what had been a relatively paltry $12.4 million pool put in place for 2002. "We have to find a mechanism that will ensure

---

Champions League, it might have a chance of winning the big prize. Arsenal also fielded weaker teams in the early rounds of the League Cup and F.A. Cup, and rested key players even during "important" league games. Unfortunately, fans have a harder time accepting these choices than clubs and their managers do. When Manchester United famously bowed out of defending its F.A. Cup title in 1999–2000 on the grounds that it had to play in the FIFA Club Championship, the resulting firestorm convinced other clubs with similar desires that the time perhaps wasn't right for such bold thinking. Interestingly, Manchester United later claimed that it had bowed out of the F.A. Cup under pressure from the ruling Labour government. The logic behind this curious claim was that Man U had instead decided to participate in FIFA's inaugural World Club Cup competition, and the club maintained that it had done so in order to boost England's bid to host the 2006 World Cup. We all know how this worked out.

*A bad team is usually ineligible for European play, and has little hope of winning the league, so poorer teams are able to marshal their forces to make a run at either the League Cup or F.A. Cup without worrying too much about anything other than relegation.

that all players, when playing in international competitions, have adequate insurance," FIFA head Joseph "Sepp" Blatter told the press. "In principle, our regulations say the club is responsible for the insurance. But World Cup regulations also say the national team is responsible to ensure the player is decently insured. In 2006 we have this special insurance pool that if a player is injured, and his insurance costs are not covered, the costs will be covered by this special fund."

This may not protect FIFA. Before the World Cup started, Belgian side Charleroi, with the support of the so-called Group of 14 super clubs (which actually number eighteen), sued Morocco's national team over damages to midfielder Abdelmajid Oulmers that they said cost some $800,000. Prior to the Cup, the G-14 went on record as saying it costs the organization between $1 and $2 billion to release players for national team games (which is a crock), so it's unlikely FIFA's move will really make headway. This proposal was floated in the same week the G-14 met with some twenty-five other clubs to discuss "representation" and "a seat at the table" . . . which to UEFA means "breakaway" and "the destruction of national team football."

Conveniently, the G-14 released a study of its own. It's proposing an expansion of the Champions League to forty-eight teams; doubling the frequency of the continental championships and the World Cup; and, oh yes, by the way, playing the World Club Cup (FIFA's baby, not the G-14's) just once every four years. In truth, the hubbub is about the clubs wanting some of the money that FIFA and UEFA suck in like slop from a trough. But it is also about national team football and the fact that the big clubs would rather cherry-pick talent than develop it.

While England was obsessing over a foot, other countries were doing their own soul-searching. Italy's soccer-loving public was coming to grips with a major corruption scandal in its sport. Entering the tournament as nominal favorites (along with Argentina, Germany, and Brazil), Italy had been rocked by reports that some big teams had "arranged" referee assignments for their games. Four clubs would be investigated and punished in the aftermath, with Juventus being relegated a division and AC Milan having its *scudetti** stripped for the past two seasons. During the scandal Juventus's director of sport, Gianluca Pessotto, attempted suicide by leaping from a fourth-floor window; his wife later claimed the attempt was due to personal problems. Goalkeeper Gianluigi Buffon was firmly questioned by the authorities over whether he had bet on games (he had, but maintained not on ones he played in, a variation of the Pete Rose defense) and would finally be cleared well after the Cup. Italians widely thought this would be a killing blow to their chance to hoist a fourth Cup.

In Germany, the home fans found even more to fret about in their team. Their coach, former World Cup winner (in 1990) Juergen Klinsmann, was viewed with deep suspicion by the powers that be. For one thing, he lived in America, with an American wife, one Debbie Chin. For another, he preferred America to Germany and made no bones about it. He had been hammered publicly by World Cup organizer Franz Beckenbauer and members of the German federation for various perceived infractions—hiring American sports psychologists and fitness trainers, and lingering in California—and until the Germans pummeled the USA in Dort-

*The *scudetto* is the name given to the top Italian league's season and title.

mund the mood toward him was downright hostile. If you're thinking the problem was that he seemed "too American," you're on target. Despite a run of fine play leading up to the Cup, Germans remained grim about their team as kickoff approached. Germany's final pre-Cup warm-up game was met with a reaction best described as: "We beat Colombia handily. We are very bad."

On the street, the concerns were a bit different. In Bad Kissingen, fans were startled to be greeted by a screaming man in drag and on stilts. A part of the Ecuadorean troupe, he introduced the team surrounded by performers in traditional costume. An Andean band with guitars and pipes played throughout the game. Such cheer unnerved many here, especially when it was accompanied with broad grins, big, unexpected hugs, and slurred requests in Spanish to take your picture with them.

Similar problems occurred in Munich, where the hot topic was the cheery groups of Costa Rican fans wobbling in and out of the beer gardens, and how to avoid them. "It does not matter whether we win or lose tomorrow," Ticos fan Luis Alvarez told me. "We are here, and we can win the [following] two games. It would be good for Germany to win their first game. It would get everyone excited." The Ticos also boasted a six-piece band, flags, scarves, and an entourage of about a hundred fans, some enterprisingly carrying banners emblazoned not with the Costa Rican flag but with ads for the restaurants they owned back home! It seemed the band members knew only one tune, but they gamely played it again and again for camera crews, radio stations, and their own "newsmen," who were, in reality, guys yelling loudly into cell phones, "calling the action" for radio stations back home.

"Now if only they had a team, too," cracked one English gent as he walked by.

However, the Germans would get even for all the joie de vivre. The ebullient Costa Ricans were stunned by the fact that bits of Munich's public parks are given over to casual nudity. In fact, if you were riding around on one of the little bikes the DB* giddily handed over to foreign journalists, sooner or later, you'd likely roll right over some nude man. Sadly, the nude folks, they were almost always men.† This horrified the Costa Rican women and emboldened the Costa Rican men with somewhat predictable results; soon there were nude men yelling at one another in at least three languages. Have I mentioned it was freezing out? In late May it was windy, it was raining, and some bits of the country even got a little snow. Why were these people naked?

The beloved Tico Marching Band expanded to include dancers as the night dragged on. They were the hit of the Viktualiemarkt, even as their hangers-on behavior became more erratic. (Okay, let's be honest: falling-down drunk.) But a happy set of drunks they were, neatly returning each glass for a refill while using progressively more inventive "German" with the bartenders. The best part: One guy behind the taps happened to be from Spain, and understood them perfectly. He was having a blast gently messing with 'em.

Then there was the ever-popular World Cup as Seen by the South Koreans. Indefatigable Korean fans, dressed in their

---

*The German railroad. What bicycles have to do with trains is beyond me as well.
†See the footnote on p. 70. Should you visit, you may wish to stress to your travel agent that you are not a gay sex tourist. Unless, of course, you are. Did I mention the central location of my wonderful flat?

usual "Be the Reds" gear, alighted in Cologne, Germany, to discover the streets were not full of cheering fans and, in fact, most people didn't seem to care. This stunned them, and many of them told passersby they hoped the next World Cup would be in South Korea as a result. "When we sing our anthem, Dae-Han-Min-Guk, no one joins in," one of them told a Korean reporter there. "People kept telling us to keep it down on the train. It was strange they didn't want to enjoy themselves." This was nothing, however, compared to what happened when the South Korean team alighted. Thousands of screaming fans kept the team bus from moving more than a few inches at a time. It took two hours for the bewildered players to get inside the hotel, and that was only after hotel security had largely given up any hope of containing the team.

I took pleasure in watching German TV sportscasters (who set a new level for rudeness to their colleagues) reduced to covering a liquor company event when they couldn't get close to the Brazilian team. After waiting a frightfully long time not to talk to Ronaldo, they glumly settled for four scantily clad and strategically placed Brazilian dames who told their hosts how to mix up a caipirinha.* In Portuguese. Our hosts instead packed up and headed off to the nearest beer garden. Rather ungrateful, especially after the kind ladies offered them the drinks with two straws.

---

*The caipirinha, a concoction of limes, sugar, and a sugarcane-derived alcohol called *cahaça,* is the so-called national drink of Brazil. To make one, muddle the limes well in a short glass with two teaspoons of sugar. Fill the glass with ice and then the *cahaça.* As cahaça is uncommon outside of Brazil, you can also substitute clear rum. You will find it both strong and delicious. Recommended dosage: Two.

This gleeful nonsense would spread throughout the nation. In Berlin, the media wouldn't even get a shot at work—their headquarters were evacuated after a piece of a World War II–era bomb was found on the grounds. Still, some gamely reported the wonderful tidbit that the police were abandoning their plans to have direct contact with fans should any "police actions" be warranted. The plan was to put fans at ease by using colloquial language and humor over a loudspeaker; the hitch turned out to be that these speeches were to be delivered in German, which most of the fans didn't understand.

Berlin was perhaps also grieving the loss of a major opera production. *Soccersongs,* a frankly bizarre collaboration between the director Robert Wilson and the composer Herbert Groenemeyer, had to be canceled due to financial shortfalls. The first scene was to have been a soccer match with dinosaurs; the second would have added cavewomen into the mix. "It will be an event for the family," said Wilson dryly at a news conference. You can't make this stuff up.

Over in Bonn, giddy at getting the Japanese team to stay there, the mayor was forced to ask excitable Japanese fans please not to dive into the Rhine. Apparently, it's fast, and they might drown. And Japan's mascot, nicknamed "Ron" (short for "Rommel"), a pain-in-the-ass canine, was the toast of the town. No one pointed out how tasteless it was to bring a dog named Rommel to a German World Cup.

Whatever country you supported, the hot accoutrement for nighttime revels in Germany was the Mohawk. Throughout the city of Munich fans by the hundreds had purchased a hairpiece in their nation's colors. It was marketing genius—tough bits of old, worn-out wig sprayed in three colors; all yours for €15. While the wig probably did not do much for a fan's chances of getting a date, it was a talking point, as well as a good old-fashioned point-and-laugh gadget, and there were a lot of folks doing both.

The night before the kickoff, the streets in Munich's old city center filled. Men dressed in peculiar-colored suits and wearing large credentials took over the Marienplatz, where a giant stage had been set up to accommodate the city's official kickoff for the World Cup. Like so many things with the word "official" in them, this would actually be a group of people on a dais, talking. No one paid any attention to them.

The English fans, dressed snazzily, if tastelessly, in World War I–era German helmets, had spent most of the day trying to outdrink the Costa Ricans, who, in turn, had already out-drunk the Tunisians, at least one of whom was passed out under a table. Both groups were singing the "Olé Olé" song, though one of them was only singing it in an attempt to drown out the folks on the stage. They did a fine job of it, despite the soundman's continued efforts to try to do his own job and the interference of the lone, overzealous South Korean fan and his large flag.

As a heartwarming film about poor nations playing soccer unspooled behind the speakers, folks took the opportunity to hit the Ratskeller for more beer and sausages. I saw a small, pickled group of Aussies, who justifiably wanted to play on the miniature, fenced-in Astroturf I believe was intended either for demonstrations or for restraining small children. The lone female *polizei* in charge of enforcing the no-on-the-turf rule seemed about to have a serious case of the screamies, despite what truly were incredibly charming attempts by the

Aussies to sneak around her, distract her with beer, and, in one case, drunkenly amble between her legs. How can anyone be mad at such happy folks?

Well, the Germans can. We were all supposed to pay attention to whatever that academic on stage was saying and said so well for so long that at one point one of his counterparts seemed to drift into a fugue. There is a certain dignity to be upheld at these things. None of us should have been distracted by the family who slept in their car to get there from Poland, and who dressed their newborn up in a tiny Polish kit. None of us should have taken the Aussies up on their beer-bong dare, nor should we have cheered them when they finally ripped the tiny fence away from the tiny patch of turf. Nor should my head, in particular, have repeatedly swerved in that arcane wife-alerting motion toward the Brazilian samba girls.

As the streets teemed, all of Germany descended into gleeful chaos. I made my way to my flat, through a pack of Dutch fans wearing bright orange Viking helmets and long lederhosen, sending up two stereotypes with one blow. I turned on the TV to see a quarter of a million fans partying at the Brandenburg Gate in what was the biggest mass demonstration Berlin had seen since the fall of the Wall.

I'd be kept up all night by fireworks and drunken fans, as some Germans vainly tried to retain some semblance of order.

They would fail. The World Cup was here.

IT'S ALL GOING OFF

At the U-Bahn stop near my rented flat the newsagent asked, "Are you here for the World Cup?"

"Why, yes, how can you tell?"

"Your German is terrible."

Ah, Munich—the capital of Bavaria, and the kickoff city for the World Cup finals, where fretting is a favorite pastime and the Cup's slogan* was distinctly ironic.

This isn't to suggest that all Germans were inhospitable, or that visitors didn't have a good time, but tensions lay beneath the frivolities. Germany, with unemployment rates of up to 20 percent in some areas, was still struggling with the reintegration of the formerly Communist Eastern bloc and deeply concerned about a rising tide of anti-immigrant and nationalistic feeling. Thanks to a semihysterical media that had primed Germany with an inexorable drumbeat over the threat of terrorism, prostitution, white slavery and trafficking, Polish

---

*"A time to make friends," if you've forgotten.

hoodlums,* stadium safety, match-fixing scandals,† and corruption in the Bundesliga, the country was already at a boiling
point the week before the Cup. Headlines in the tabloids went
for the throat: One read THE EASTERN NEO-NAZIS ARE COMING!;
another newspaper decried the orgy of fans spilling into the
cities with a simple MAKE IT STOP! No wonder former national
team star and manager and current World Cup organizer Franz
Beckenbauer dryly noted, "We [Germans] are unfortunately
not perceived as a particularly friendly people." He had already
issued a call to his countrymen to smile for their visitors. "It is
only for a few weeks," he pleaded.

Was this paranoia or just fatigue? It was impossible to get away
from the Cup, after all. Some halfhearted attempts were made

---

*In 2006 Germany's problems included its very geography. Both the eco-
nomic center of Europe and astraddle the cold war's dividing line, the nation
was about to host a tournament full of old enemies and, prior to kickoff, the
presence of organized thugs invading the Cup was a real worry. The German
government had legitimate security concerns about subsets of Polish, English, Czech, Serbian, and Dutch fans. Some foreigners were even warned
against travel into the eastern regions of the nation, which had seen an up-
swing in neo-Nazi activity. The far-right NPD (Nationaldemokratische
Partei Deutschlands) planned to march through Gelsenkirchen after the
Ecuador vs. Poland game on June 10, as well as a rally in support of Iran's
openly anti-Israel president, Mahmoud Ahmadinejad, in Leipzig on June 21.
Though there was some racist behavior among fans (and not all German
ones, by any stretch—the Serbs were real beauts to be around), neither event
came to pass, yet both received wide publicity before the Cup.
†A major and deeply embarrassing match-fixing scandal involving a referee
named Robert Hoyzer had broken in February of 2005. Hoyzer rigged a series of matches in conjunction with a Croat gambling syndicate. He was
caught and sentenced to two years and five months in jail, but the scandal
lingered. The feeling that there were other perpetrators who eluded capture
due to the scandal's proximity to the World Cup did not improve Germany's tense atmosphere—or German football's reputation.

in the so-called Fussballfrie zones, and for reasons that would never be made clear, this short-lived movement promised to stage an "antifootball" march on the night of the Berlin final. A few cafés and bars hung placards on their fronts promising shelter from TV and radio. But there was no escape from conversations, screaming headlines, and the packs of fans.

Unquestionably the 2006 edition was the most pimped World Cup ever staged and FIFA president Blatter was compelled to deny suggestions that it was "too commercial." These denials were hard to believe when every few feet in Germany you were confronted by a World Cup ad, a World Cup licensed product, or something salable in the shape of a soccer ball. The soccer-ball waffles: very good; the soccer-ball sausage: poison. In the center of Munich's commercial district, every window was made up as a fake field, every mannequin wore a strip, and every product—no matter how remote—was given a temporary World Cup makeover.

Take the ghastly ceramic clowns playing football, on sale at the department store a hundred feet from the U-Bahn exit. Ceramic clowns are naturally ghastly, but to see them contorted into bicycle kicks or leaping "King Kahn" saves* was a whole new level of horrid. Then there were the plants. If an African violet in, well, violet, wasn't good enough, you could have it sprayed yellow, red, and black. Did I mention the caps that looked like deflated soccer balls? These were especially useless: They invited someone to take a kick at your head but did nothing to protect you from sun or rain. I saw a pair of morose Brazil fans walking around wearing these, undoubtedly on orders from their mother.

---

*Named after cast-off German captain and goalkeeper Oliver Kahn.

The nadir came with World Cup–branded sex toys. As it happens, there were not one but two sex shops near my flat, which made me wonder what my travel agent thought of me,* and I could well have become the proud owner of a soccer-ball-patterned vibrator. I was told these should not be used on "unexplained calf pain," but the shop owner agreed with me that, in all likelihood, no one has ever gone right for her calves with one of these foot-long devices. However, things are different here: June's German edition of *Playboy* had soccer balls on its shiny green cover instead of the usual half-naked coed. Apparently German men are more turned on by the thought of soccer than by scantily clad women. Could this be why everyone's so depressed?

It was too much. At the supermarket, I saw people go out of their way to avoid buying World Cup tie-in items. One guy tore through a whole pyramid of bottled water just to get one without Michael Ballack's mug on it. I couldn't have been the only one who felt it was just deserts that the maker of the Goleo mascot toys went bankrupt on the eve of the tournament. Sales were poor because the idiotic lion mascot was revolting, a cheap rip-off of the iconic World Cup Willie from England 1966. Also, parts of the toys turned out to be toxic.

Still, I could understand why Germany's organizers were tempted to slap a logo and price tag on everything. In Korea and Japan people positively gloried in this stuff; folks there dressed head to toe in World Cup–branded regalia and stood

---

*I would come to discover that I was not only lodged in the gay district but surrounded by Asian-staffed brothels as well. Did I mention the apartment was superb and centrally located?

in huge lines to buy more. And German businesses needed to make a dime off the Cup. I don't think it's any wonder the Cup had some tension. Hanging over everyone's heads were history, money, and fear.

The three major sporting events that Germany had staged prior to the 2006 World Cup were the 1936 Berlin Olympic Games, the ill-fated 1972 Olympic Games in Munich, and the 1974 World Cup.

The 1974 World Cup was one of the first tournaments to demonstrate the power of world television and was certainly a precursor to the TV-dominated 2006 edition. And certainly the worlds of 1972 and 2006 have similarities—unpopular American presidents fighting ill-considered wars, a global energy crisis, a war raging in the Middle East. However, the tournament that most closely paralleled the 2006 World Cup was the Berlin Olympic Games. German readers will likely take umbrage with this, but both events were used by the German government to present a "new" Germany to the world;* both events took place during times of financial hardship and ethnic tension; and both tournaments were staged by groups that largely turned a blind eye to some of the seamier aspects of the events they were staging.

There's no equivalency between the despicable, willful blindness of the International Olympic Committee (IOC) toward the persecution of Germany's Jewish population in 1936—the IOC wasn't just hoodwinked by the Nazis, it was

---

*For more on this subject, please see Guy Walters's *Berlin Games* (William Morrow and Co./HarperCollins, 2006).

almost complicit—and the venality and posturing of FIFA in 2006.* However, the Cup's presence in Germany was itself mildly scandalous. That it was awarded to Germany was proof to some that the core of FIFA, with its bleating about "fair play for all," was fundamentally rotten. (For others, the award to Germany was unsurprising after the money-sink that was the 2002 World Cup.) The campaign to get it had eerie overtones of how the German government had politicked shamelessly for a major event in the hopes of presenting a new face . . . in 1936.

To understand fully the controversy behind the choice of a host country, it's useful to know some of the history of the selection process, and more about the money at stake. The World Cup didn't come into existence until 1928, when a small group of Frenchmen dreamed of a global showcase for the sport. And why not? The game had spread like wildfire through the British, Spanish, and Portuguese empires, giving the game outposts in South America, Africa, and even Shanghai. In fact, the World Cup was not the first international soccer tournament, nor was it the second or third: Soccer was a part of the 1908 Olympic Games in London and would be a mainstay of the competition for two decades. Until the 1932 Olympic Games in the United States (where soccer was dropped due to American indifference) the Olympics was the pinnacle of soccer competition. There had been global club

---

*CONCACAF head Jack Warner got caught trying to sell World Cup tickets and travel to the impoverished people of Trinidad and Tobago at a fierce markup. He wasn't the only one, but he was just one of two folks who got caught. On December 6, 2006, Warner was "scolded" by FIFA for this, but not punished. The other man, Ismail Bhamjee of Botswana, was not so lucky. He was expelled from the Cup. See page 121.

competitions as well. In 1909, and then again in 1911, the enterprising Sir Thomas Lipton, a Scottish tea magnate, staged interclub tournaments in Italy to decide the "world's best."*

But Jules Rimet and his fellow organizers of the inaugural World Cup decided that Olympic-only soccer just wouldn't do; they proposed a sixteen-team field, to play in 1930. Uruguay, which won the gold medal in both the 1924 and 1928 Olympics, was considered the unofficial world champion at the time by the still-young FIFA, and as a result, when FIFA decided to hold its first sanctioned world championship, it awarded it to the South American country.

This turned out to be something of a mistake. Due to the expense and difficulty of traveling from Europe to South America, only four teams from the Old World—Belgium, France, Yugoslavia, and Romania—accepted the invitation to attend. Another seven teams from South America—Argentina, Chile, Uruguay, Brazil, Bolivia, Peru, and Paraguay— were joined by the United States and Mexico. That was the best Rimet could do, so the 1930 World Cup kicked off with just thirteen teams. Because of the uneven number of teams, some nations played more games than others—Brazil, for example, played six times, while eventual champions Uruguay played only four.

Rimet solved that problem for the next edition of the Cup, staging it in Italy. With this tournament, two new factors came into play. First, with thirty-two teams entering, there were "qualifying rounds" that winnowed the field to sixteen. Second, and more important perhaps, politics entered

---

*Lipton later moved on to greater fame as a consistent challenger for yachting's America's Cup.

the World Cup. These games, staged and won under Benito Mussolini's Fascist rule, are widely considered to have been as politicized and stage-managed as the 1936 Olympic Games in Berlin. Dictator Mussolini pressured referee Ivan Eklind to give the home side favorable treatment and it worked, as Italy won the first of its four Cups.

Following the 1934 Cup, the tournament began to meander around the globe; it has now been staged in every continent save Africa and the collection of islands called Oceania.

Tellingly, more people today will watch a World Cup match than will celebrate Earth Day or Christmas. Just when the Cup became a planetary obsession is open to debate. Anglophiles will point to 1966 as the year the World Cup became a global event (because England won it, naturally), but the reality is that the tournament really showed its muscles with the West German edition of 1974 and the advent of satellite-enabled closed-circuit television. Suddenly, World Cup games could be seen live around the world and, better yet, sold for a handsome price. In one fell swoop this shrewd move gave FIFA an enormous revenue stream, and the organization has continued to set the bar for rights fees in global televised sports.*

This revenue allowed FIFA to consolidate its power using a byzantine and perhaps deliberately obscure manner of dis-

---

*In fact, only the NFL sucks up as much money in one fell swoop, but the NFL is hamstrung by the fact that its audience is largely limited to the United States. Efforts to popularize American football in Europe and in other countries—such as Japan and Mexico—have met with mixed results. Growth for an NFL franchise has been estimated at about 3 percent a year; a soccer club can show growth that is many times that. As a result, a number of NFL owners (Cleveland's Randy Lerner and Tampa Bay's Malcolm Glazer being the best known) have either purchased European franchises outright or are investigating partnerships.

persing funds to various nations for "improvements" in the sport. Some countries in the modern era have clearly benefited from these efforts—Jamaica and Barbados have both been able to transfer football revenues into new grounds and infrastructure—but there remains a great gap between the traditional powers in the sport and the rest of the world.

Along the way, FIFA has been careful to do one thing above all: pretend that it has no personal interest. FIFA maintains that it is nothing more than a steward of the game of soccer. This has allowed FIFA to concentrate resources and firepower on one region at a time in an effort both to lay down roots for the game and to establish a stranglehold on the money that comes along as a result. FIFA started this process in Europe, moved to South America and Africa, and is currently dabbling in the United States and Asia. FIFA continues to resist any governmental attempts to regulate its power and jealously guards its trademarks. Of late, FIFA, rapaciously watching member organization UEFA make a killing with the European Champions League club competition, announced it would hold its own World Club Championships before anyone else could beat it to it. The first was staged in Brazil, and it was a notable flop; the jury remains out on the revived edition, staged in Japan.

For a tournament with such global reach, the World Cup is a remarkably closed shop. It has long been dominated by the "traditional powers" (along the European and South American axis) and only seven nations have ever won the title: Brazil (a five-time winner and defending champion in 2006), Germany (a three-time winner as West Germany), Italy (four wins), Argentina (two), Uruguay (two), England (one), and France (one).

Nonetheless, FIFA has grown the World Cup from a parochial competition into an economic engine second to none in the sports world. Unlike the Olympics, which have famously bankrupted host cities, the World Cup usually ends up making money. The teams are paid, FIFA gets a whale of a cut, and despite huge spending on infrastructure, even countries such as Korea get a little bump.* This is unique in modern sports, at least according to economists who study sports finance. In fact, those economists, given to patiently, accurately, and vociferously detailing how most spending on American sports is never recouped (usually around the time an American pro team is searching for a new stadium), look at the World Cup with something approaching admiration. The Cup not only builds up cities, it makes people rich. What could be better?

Let's talk about that cash a little bit. Money drives modern sports, and the World Cup is no exception. The Cup is also the most-watched event in the television age: Six times the population of the planet tuned in to Germany 2006. Rights fees for the Cup give FIFA billions of dollars per cycle. In America, ESPN/ABC paid a reported $130 million for the rights to 2006 and 2010 (which were part of a package that included other, considerably less popular FIFA events, including the next Women's World Cup). This fee is actually low. In

---

*Down the road is a different story. Many of the stadiums South Korea built for the 2002 World Cup now lie empty on a regular basis. Initially intended to house other events and become home ground for teams in South Korea's national league, the "K-League," the buildings have, for a confluence of factors—including the arenas' grand sizes and the locales—become white elephants.

comparison, in the same market, the Spanish-language tele-cast rights cost Univision $180 million.* Such fees help ex-plain why there was something of a scandal when it was revealed that FIFA had once "sold" the Caribbean rights to a group controlled by Jack Warner, a FIFA vice president and the head of the region's governmental body, CONCACAF. FIFA's price for the insider? One dollar.

The World Cup, if you believed FIFA's accounting, would earn the organization $144 million on turnover of $1.64 bil-lion in revenue in the four-year cycle that led up to and in-cluded the 2006 World Cup. According to people who currently work in the organization and people who have worked for FIFA at other World Cups and in other capacities, that stated amount is almost certainly low. FIFA conducts many of its dealings in cash, so it is impossible to tell just how much money is going in and out at any given time.

These internal machinations are probably of little interest to the casual fan. However, there is one financial fact about the World Cup that does affect the hosts and the event: All of the money the Cup makes from TV goes right back into FIFA's big pockets to be distributed out to the participating teams (who earn a minimum of $1 million a game for playing plus a onetime bonus of $12 million for qualifying) with the sur-plus then socked away in Swiss accounts. FIFA contributes nothing to the staging of the Cup itself, or to all the "improve-ments" FIFA requires countries to make to their stadiums,

---

*It should be noted that the seller of the World Cup rights—a group called Soccer United Marketing, which is an offshoot of the American soccer league MLS—claim that the Americas spend more money in TV rights fees to FIFA for the World Cup than any other region in the world.

roads, hotels, and so on. The hosts must hope that the increased tourism, prestige, and retail sales offset those costs.

In fact, FIFA, save for collecting the cash, is surprisingly hands-off when it comes to the staging of the Cup. From the stadium openings and turf conditions to making sure the subways run on time, the behind-the-scenes details of the Cup are the host's responsibility.* The result is a terrible burden for the host countries, who see their lives made miserable by FIFA's rather snarky reviews of the proceedings. A popular entertainment during the 2006 run-up was following along in the papers as Joseph Blatter lobbed near-daily verbal jabs at an exasperated Franz Beckenbauer. Part of that was political— Blatter is a cutthroat pol who is canny enough not to let someone successfully stage a Cup and then use that as a platform to challenge him for his job with FIFA. But, over the years, I've come to realize that part of it is just for the sheer joy of tormenting people. There's a real mean streak in FIFA, and it's never far from the surface. The fact of the matter is, FIFA isn't risking its own cash, despite grandiose talk of how much funding the Cup "puts back into football." The truth is the German government and taxpayers bore almost all the hard costs of the 2006 Cup.

FIFA, which isn't stupid, knows that potential hosts understand this, at least initially. FIFA sells the event to skeptics

---

*Appearances notwithstanding, FIFA leaves nothing to chance. They insinuate every level of the Local Organizing Committee (LOC), and their "experts" consult and/or bedevil (take your pick) every aspect of the Cup's planning. When the tournament starts, the LOC is forced to take a back seat to FIFA ops crews, media officers, marketing people, and so forth. This gives FIFA wonderful deniability and causes real headaches for the LOC, for if something goes wrong, despite the fact that FIFA's been enmeshed from day one, FIFA just blames the LOC and most folks believe them.

with the stagecraft, grandeur, and potential prestige of the event. If the host countries forget along the way that this rhetoric is a *sales pitch,* there can be uncomfortable consequences.

A good demonstration of this at its worst was the 2003 Women's World Cup, the second to be hosted in the United States. Unlike the wildly successful 1999 event, this tournament was a clusterfuck from the word go: The original host, China, had to bow out due to the SARS epidemic and the hastily scheduled tournament went up against the NFL, the World Series, and college football. Though the United States was a last-minute step-in savior, the disappointment when the Cup didn't even come close to meeting the 1999 version was very real. The aftermath has seen the women's game in the United States fall off a cliff. The women's professional league, WUSA, folded on the eve of the tourney and has never been able to come back, and the attention given the women's team since can be measured in centimeters of newsprint. (In July 2006, the *San Diego Union-Tribune* published an article by Mark Zeigler, one of the better correspondents on the game, about this subject with the telling headline: WHERE HAS THE LOVE GONE?)*

But the World Cup can also have a broader, and perhaps more sinister, reach. Because of the attention now paid to the Cup, it has the power to alter the fabric of the societies it visits. Make no mistake: *This* is the force nations attempt to harness every four years, and for their own devices. Under the canopy of a myth, a lot of things can and do happen—for better or for ill.

---

*Just prior to the publication of this book, plans were announced for a new women's pro league to kick off in 2008. The announcement was met with skepticism, as opposed to enthusiasm. As of publication, it is unclear whether this league will come to pass.

In America's case, the 1994 men's World Cup paved the way for the sport to succeed as a professional entertainment. The catch that the nascent Major League Soccer has yet to figure a way around is that the Cup also became a model that is almost impossible for a league to equal. As a result, the sport continues to weather tough times.

In England, that country's lone win in 1966 trapped it in a vicious cycle of high expectations and real failures. Despite a hugely successful league, the Premiership, England's national team seems cursed to disappoint; wins are magnified beyond belief and losses are dissected with a cruelty that is almost sadistic.

At the Asian Cup, despite FIFA's pitch that football could be a uniting force, both South Korea and Japan experienced an increase in fervent nationalism, revealing some characteristics that had been long-buried. Today, one of Japan's top-selling books is a manga called *Hating the Korean Wave*. It begins with a chapter detailing how South Korea "cheated" to finish above Japan at the Cup. It has sold close to seven hundred thousand copies.

In the run-up to 2006, Germany hoped for the opportunity to show the rest of the planet that the de facto bank of Europe could be a nice place to visit or perhaps to relocate a business or two. In the midst of political and social upheaval, enduring a stagnant economy with high unemployment, Germans and German politicians didn't just hope hosting the World Cup could spur some change in their bottom line— they were desperate.

However, the competition to host the 2006 Cup didn't start out in an atmosphere of cynicism, but with the idealistic hopes of independent South Africa, which was presenting itself as a candidate for the first time. South Africa's motivations for wanting to host the Cup were, to be fair, much the same as Germany's: The African nation had just gone through a reunification process of its own following the collapse of the brutal apartheid regime. A staple of the black townships, soccer was a contributor to the collapse of the apartheid system, with its teams acknowledged as providing a valuable channel for political discussion and organized resistance.

Represented by the charismatic Danny Jordaan, South Africa's bid to host the World Cup was simple. It took FIFA on its official line—that the sport was a bridge between cultures—and called the organization on it. South Africa had little to offer a World Cup in the way of financial support, but it carried a huge club: shame. A number of FIFA's major members had demonstrated real ambivalence during the apartheid years, and others had explicitly broken the economic and sporting embargoes imposed on the country, undermining what was supposed to be a global effort. The classic example is the staging of tours by so-called wildcat cricket teams from England. These teams toured South Africa with such regularity that it is difficult to imagine they were not tacitly supported.*

---

*Four tours of English "select XI's" (unsanctioned national teams) organized by Coventry City football club chairman Derek Robins visited the country between 1973 and 1976 alongside a women's select from New Zealand and a polyglot team based out of Rhodesia. The multinational "International Wanderers" also played in 1976. Following an outbreak of civil strife, four so-called rebel teams—two from England and two from the West Indies—toured in the 1980s. Those later rebel teams were punished: The English player Graham Gooch served a three-year ban while the West Indian players took life bans. The final tour, a financial disaster, also resulted in a three-year ban for former England captain Mike Gatting.

So when it was announced that South Africa was willing and able to host the 2006 Cup, FIFA jumped at the chance. No one was more enthusiastic than the president. Blatter openly touted the South African bid, saying it was "time the sport returned to Africa." It seemed like South Africa was a lock.

But that isn't the way things work in world sports. First came an interminable round of handshaking and bowing and scraping, most notably in the case of Warner. The CONCA-CAF president requested that Nelson Mandela, aging and unwell at the time, visit him at his compound in Trinidad. After a semi-humiliating round of scrapage, in which the poor man was apparently trucked across the islands, Mandela did secure CONCACAF's support for the South African Cup.

But when it came time for the vote, Germany emerged as a last-second alternate, arguing that Europe needed representation after a 2002 Cup that would be held outside the "home of the game." It was also pointed out to FIFA executives that South Africa was a country in financial chaos, and the rich proceeds the group has come to expect would not be forthcoming. And Blatter, though perhaps not the FIFA Executive, knew that FIFA's longtime sports marketing partner, ISL/ISM, was on the verge of financial collapse, and about to take with it a sizable chunk of FIFA's money.*

---

*Prior to the 2002 World Cup, several high-ranking FIFA officials, led by Blatter's own deputy, Michel Zen-Ruffinen, alleged that the collapse of ISL/ISM had led to losses approaching $100 million under Blatter's tenure. These allegations of financial mismanagement were backed by Blatter's political nemesis Lennart Johansson, the president of UEFA (Europe's governing body for the sport), but after a nasty public spat Zen-Ruffinen was removed from office and Blatter quashed an investigation into the matter. In 2006 the BBC investigative program *Panorama,* in conjunction with journalist Andrew Jennings, renewed some of these allegations, detailing how

What happened next is in dispute. According to Andrew Jennings, who has written a long book about it called *Foul!,** FIFA schemed to appear to support the South African bid while ensuring the tournament went to the far-richer Germany. What is known, however, is that South Africa lost the 2006 tournament by one vote, because the delegate from Oceania abstained.

Charlie Dempsey[†] was that man, a taut old boy said to have a somewhat abrasive manner and a taste for hooch. Dempsey had been ordered to vote for South Africa by his bosses, and his vote would have likely been decisive. The Executive was evenly split down the middle twelve–twelve, and a tie would have forced Blatter to cast the tie-breaking vote. Instead, Dempsey walked out, leaving the vote at twelve–eleven, a figure that, when initially flashed in the South African bid offices, made no sense to the observers. How could only twenty-three votes be tallied when there were twenty-four members of the board?

Dempsey was soon back on a plane to Oceania, where he would be relieved of his duties. He offered a strange justification for abstaining, claiming he had been harassed and was the target of attempted bribes.

Blatter had rigged votes to consolidate his power. Jennings's book, *Foul!* (HarperCollinsWillow, 2007), drew a strong denial from FIFA when it was published to coincide with the program's airing during the 2006 World Cup. According to two people familiar with the inner workings of FIFA, Jennings's book is largely accurate in its portrayals.

*FIFA went to court to block *Foul!*'s publication, but failed in its attempt. Jennings obligingly reproduces some amusingly Orwellian correspondence from FIFA's lawyers at the end of the book, which is a must-read for fans of doublespeak.

[†]For the record, Charlie Dempsey is no relation to Clint Dempsey, the American midfielder.

"[This] final fax broke my neck," complained Dempsey. "I chose to abstain because of the intolerable pressure that was put on me by all. Not by the actual bidding people, but the people on the fringe and incessant phone calls that I was receiving in my room, and also the attempts to bribe me."

It turned out this final fax was actually a hoax by the German satirical magazine *Titanic*. Editor Martin Sonneborn and his staff had apparently sent seven FIFA committee members faxes offering ham, sausages, a beer mug, and a "wonderful KuKuClock" if the committee members voted for Germany.* And one of the phone calls Dempsey was referring to was from none other than Mandela, a man who just about anyone in the world would be happy to take a call from, at any time!

Predictably, this resulted in a hot controversy. In the wake of it, FIFA agreed to rotate the tournament through the continents, giving South Africa the 2010 tournament.† But the damage had been done. The tournament billed as "a time to make friends" began with a squabble that had fans, with some cause, suggesting the Europeans were afraid of giving Africa a chance. Others hinted at darker, racially motivated reasons. Jennings writes that it simply came down to money. We are unlikely ever to know the truth. But we do know this:

In the aftermath of the vote, Jordaan addressed the crowd at a ballroom at the Baur au Lac Hotel in Zurich. Never mentioning the politics of division that had led to South Africa's loss, Jordaan praised everyone for the effort and ended his

*Sonneborn told all in a book about the experience and recounted it for *Der Spiegel* as well just prior to the World Cup.
†Despite denials from FIFA and South Africa's organizing committee, financial hardships may result in the 2010 Cup being relocated to either Australia or North America.

speech by leading his audience in a rendition of the new South African national anthem, "Nkosi Sikelel' iAfrika." It was one of the most moving moments in the sport's history.

When the time came, the tensions between past and present that Germany was trying to reconcile with its presentation of the Cup made Munich an ideal location for its opening night.

Munich, observed Thomas Mann, glows. Nearly 850 years old, the city is one of the architectural marvels of Europe, a baroque and rococo playground dominated by fantastic monumental buildings. Bedecked with bright colors, stone Bavarian lions, and a marvelous eighteenth-century city center, the Altstadt, Munich has long been considered the Athens of Germany.

Munich was the seat of Bavarian kings, built on wealth from the region's monopoly on salt mining. It prided itself on things we think of today as typically "German": the lush beer gardens and artists' fairs of summer, the universities that transformed education from a privilege for the rich into a right for the masses, the open-air markets. And Munich has always been a center for commerce, tourism, and pleasure. Whole parts of the city were explicitly planned with tourists in mind:* The Altstadt is almost entirely pedestrian, the massive Englischer Garten is one of the world's largest parks, and the almost garish Rathaus-Glockenspiel in the Marienplatz has delighted children and their parents for centuries with its mechanical dancers.

However, there is another Munich. The city was the birthplace and spiritual home of the National Socialist Party—the

---

*The city's official motto is the saccharine "Munich Loves You."

Nazis. Adolf Hitler rose to prominence and power here, using Munich's vibrant culture to his advantage by selling his message through speeches given at public halls and beer gardens, as well as through a newspaper his party had purchased. While Hitler's first attempt at seizing power, the Beer Hall Putsch of 1923, failed, his subsequent imprisonment and the publication of *Mein Kampf* set the stage for things to come.

During the Third Reich, large parts of Munich were given over to Nazi building projects. A whole set of buildings on the Königsplatz were erected to house the Nazi party headquarters, and from 1933 until 1939 Hitler embarked on an ambitious urban building plan that was intended ultimately to transform the city into a "FuhrerStadt," a living embodiment of the ideals of the Nazis. Many of the resulting buildings survive today, and some retain glimpses of their past. Look on the eastern wall of the former Luftgau-Kommando building to see intact wrought-iron swastikas, for example. The Haus der Kunst (Art Museum), sitting on the edge of the Englischer Garten, was designed to reflect Hitler's belief that art under the Third Reich was to be "a sublime mission owing one to fanaticism," a motto that was once engraved over the building's entrance; it was chiseled out as part of the city's "de-Nazification" process after the war. The museum was not considered a pretty building—it was nicknamed the "white sausage" by neighbors. Today Nazi architect Paul Troost's ostentatious line of Doric columns are partly camouflaged by a row of maple trees, but a peek upward inside the museum reveals the original mosaics intact, with swastikas.

There is a term for the process Germany, Munich, and Germans have undergone to reconcile themselves with their horrific past: *Vergangenheitbewältigung*. It is a phrase and a concept that has been hotly debated since the 1950s, and, depending on one's politics, it can mean "accepting the past" or "working through history" or neither or both. One thing remains clear even today, however: As other German cities have gone through agonizing examinations of their role in the Nazi era, Munich remains hesitant to break entirely with its past. I found it to be a city that has trouble dealing with its new immigrants, its tortured legacies, and the desires that brought about the Third Reich in the first place.

At the end of World War II, Allied bombing had reduced some 60 to 70 percent of Munich to rubble, and massive piles of cracked stone and iron littered the streets for years. Some of the city's finest monuments and architectural treasures were damaged almost beyond repair, and fierce debates broke out over how to rebuild the city. The city decided on what was called the Meitinger Plan, after the architect Karl Meitinger, who proposed that the old center of the city be restored to nearly its original condition, while making modern changes to the outskirts. Critics (Gavriel Rosenfeld is one) have argued that this plan tried to gloss over the Nazi era—in effect, pretending it didn't happen—and that a more ambitious plan of modernization and remembrance might have helped the city heal more thoroughly. Rosenfeld makes an interesting point, but as I walked through the city center every day, I thought how horrible it would have been had all those neoclassical and baroque buildings been replaced by modernist boxes. One of the things that makes Munich feel special is the fact that its architecture is so over-the-top and distinctive. The only place in Europe where I've found that same sort of gleeful chaos is in the old center of Brussels, a dense warren of hawkers and restaurants lining a raggedy, winding strip. Full of World Cup fans, Munich had an overwhelming, ecstatic feeling that I'm not sure could have been achieved had all the eighteenth-century buildings been swept aside.

Every morning, I could look out the window of my rented flat onto the Viktualienmarkt, Munich's enormous open-air farmers market. The giant Maypole and the beer garden would bring a smile to my face no matter how exhausted I was. I got in the fattening habit of grabbing the papers at the small stand at the back of the Altes Rathaus or at the train station and returning through the market to grab a pastry or two. Repeat and add a few sausages on the way to the day's game and you pack on the pounds in no time. The only bad thing about living there was that the Cup overlapped with asparagus season, so on some mornings the urine in the alley next to the brothel was more pungent than usual.

Munich also has some famous sporting architecture. The incredible 1974 World Cup final in which West Germany downed their greatest rival, the Netherlands, behind a late first-half goal from Gerd Müller, the "nation's Bomber," was staged here at the old Olympia Park. The Munich massacre of 1972 occurred in the same complex. Up until 2006, Bayern Munich, one of Germany's greatest club teams, made the Olympia Park its home.

Near the Olympic Park is a smaller open area, called the Luitpoldpark. It is quiet and gently banked with small hills, which is surprising considering the rest of Munich is almost entirely flat. I was impressed by how comfortable it was to sit down on one of the hills and look back over the surrounding greenery and the U-Bahn stop. I didn't find out until later that I was walking on the hidden remains of wartime Munich.

Luitpoldpark's hills are actually "Endkippens," massive piles of rubble dumped there after the war in the efforts to clear out the city. Just a few feet below the grass and trees are tons of concrete and iron, the pieces of people's homes.

The reasons I bring all this up are twofold. A city reflects the culture of the people who live in it, and architecture is the most visible representation of the collective psyche. It is easy to see why, after the horrors of the Second World War, the familiarity of a restored Altstadt would be soothing. What concerned Germans, however, was what might be forgotten in such a restoration plan. Even today, Germans are concerned that if they forget their past, they risk repeating it.

This brings up a second aspect of postwar reconstruction and healing. During the Nazi regime, citizens were compelled to fly the Nazi flag. I saw a picture of the street I stayed on, the Frauenstrasse, circa 1939, so bedecked from roof to sidewalk with the red, white, and black swastika that it was difficult to see where the flags stopped and the buildings began. No wonder, then, that in the aftermath of the war the German flag was not widely flown. Many were uneasy with nationalistic displays, well wary of the dangers of extreme pride.

The day that the 2006 World Cup kicked off, June 9, would be one of the first times since the war that Germans, especially younger ones, would fly their flag unashamedly. I sat in a restaurant with an older woman and her daughter, and we marveled at the outpouring of pride on the streets.

That afternoon, the beer gardens were full of folks, some dressed outlandishly, having a fine time drinking endless liters of beer in the blazing sun. Best costume: the dog dressed in an 1860 Munich strip and accompanied by his pet potbellied pig, which he carried in a sling. (Yes, you read that right: a dog with a pet.) Both dog and pig enjoyed a hearty lunch of dunkel* and scraps before being whisked off in the basket of their owner's scooter.

That evening, the World Cup opened with Germany taking on the famous Costa Ricans at the Allianz Arena, a large, puffy structure at the northern edge of Munich. Thanks to FIFA's sponsorship deals, the name had to be pried off the side of the building, which would be subsequently referred to as "FIFA World Cup Stadium Munich" in official documents. The arena looks like a toppled, tethered Michelin Man and while grotesque in the bright lights of day it took on a new, strange beauty at night, like a glowing UFO settling down onto the suburban hills.

As at every World Cup the opening was a time for high panic behind the scenes. FIFA had only placed eleven of its officials on the ground—a sign of confidence in the German World Cup Organizing Committee. (By contrast, FIFA will likely have to place thirty to fifty trained officers in South Africa, to say nothing of underwriting a majority of the costs of the event.) FIFA's confidence was well placed. Inside, the operation was smooth and efficient.

Unfortunately, the Munich civil government was not on the same page. For reasons that remained unexplained, Munich was unwilling to alter its ironclad train departure and arrival times, resulting in a perverse parody of German attention to detail and regulations. Fans got their first taste of the kind of mayhem this would cause throughout the entire tournament as full trains remained parked at the stations, instead

---

*A dark beer.

of moving off ahead of schedule. Because the Munich authorities apparently refused to bring enough trains into service,
enormous bottlenecks and ugly scenes developed with dangerously overfull cars and platforms at every game. Even poorly
attended matches would see ridiculous delays, compounded
by the U-Bahn's desire to close stations at the appointed hour.
Apparently it is a greater sin to add an extra train to the schedule than it is to have your station ripped apart.

Still, despite the chill that runs down your spine when
several thousand blond men step off a subway train and break
into a chant of "DEUTSCH-LAND!," the opener was a fairly
sedate event attended by as many youngsters and corporate
types as hard-core fans.

At the Allianz itself, police conducted thorough searches,
ostensibly because of the risk of terrorism. This resulted in
bottlenecks at every entrance, and a huge swath of empty seats
for the pregame show, but there were few serious incidents.
With helicopters overhead and officers on the ground on
horseback, the only problems were minor—arrests for pick-
pocketing and a drunken scuffle or two. The biggest worry of
opening day—a planned far-right demonstration—did not
materialize, but police did remove a swastika-emblazoned
banner from over the highway just prior to the game.

Inside the stadium, opening-night fans were greeted by a
short, strange pre-Cup show, featuring aerialists and Germanic techno and culminating in Toni Braxton singing the
grating official World Cup ditty, "The Time of Our Lives."
Most fans did the smart thing and drank heavily during her
three-octave, four-minute caterwaul, or crowded around the
sausage stands.

After a stuttering start, the German national team did not

disappoint its fans. Munich exploded in the sixth minute when Phillip Lahm, employing his signature move, cut from the left side into the area to sink a powerful right-footed shot into the top of José Porras's net. Lahm, who would be the only player to play every minute of every German game at the Cup, is a rare thing in football—a left-footed defender with a good right foot, giving him the ability to shift swiftly from the flanks to the center. On this goal, he caught the hapless Ticos defense—which would not impress—off balance, thanks to a bad flub by Danny Fonseca. But that should not take away from the grace and power shown in this first goal; it was a long, curling strike that no goalkeeper could have stopped and it instantly gave the German team confidence.

It should have been an easy night for the home side, but nerves played a big part: Costa Rica's Paulo Wanchope, a slowing former English Premiership player, beat the offside trap cleanly just six minutes later to slip the ball underneath the diving German goalie Jens Lehmann. Lehmann, in fact, failed to stop *any* of the Costa Ricans' forays at the net; Germany outshot the Ticos twenty-one to four but while two Costa Rican shots passed by, two—both from Wanchope—went in (giving the Ticos a strange statistical oddity: a nearly 50 percent goal-scoring ratio).

This was a tough debut for Lehmann, who had been ejected in his final club game of the year in Paris and had won a nasty, public struggle with the team's former captain, Oliver Kahn, to take the number-one job in the nets. The bitterness survives; at the time of this writing, Kahn was still telling newspapers, despite all evidence to the contrary, that Germany would have won the Cup had he been the keeper.

Thanks to the brilliance of Miroslav Klose, a Polish-born

German citizen who is a star at Bundesliga side Werder Bremen, Germany beat Costa Rica 4–2. Ironically, at the time Klose was winning the game for the Germans, Berlin police were busy seizing several thousand pieces of hate literature warning of "foreign infiltration into the national team" from the offices of the National Democratic Party.

Still, at the end, the Germans finally seemed to throw off the doubt that had plagued them for nearly six months. A beaming, sweaty Klinsmann thanked the crowd, and the World Cup was officially under way.

In Frankfurt, the first signs of trouble were surfacing. Police moved in after the airing of the first game to stop English and German fans from brawling near the train station. Forty thousand people had gathered to watch the game in the city, where England would take on Paraguay the next day. The climate was fueled by the day's unusually warm temperatures (it was in the low eighties across Germany) and by the fact that many of the English fans had mobbed an Irish pub, O'Reilly's, with a large banner proclaiming it WORLD CUP HQ. In the end, one hundred arrests were made as the second game of the day got under way in Gelsenkirschen.

There, the Poles slogged through an embarrassing 2–0 loss that all but torpedoed their hopes of reaching the next round. The game itself was a break with custom that began with the 1994 World Cup in the United States. The hosts and their opponents had traditionally played alone on the first night; now two games launch the Cup, unfortunately making the second game almost an afterthought. But for Ecuador, a battling South American country light-years away from the level of its neighbors, it was no small victory.

In China, remarkably heavy betting patterns were observed. In Indonesia and Thailand, police began to investigate the large wagers placed on the games in the hopes of catching any signs of match fixing or gaming the system. Asian soccer has been hit hard over the past decade by scandal after scandal involving legal sports betting.

In war-torn Somalia, sharia courts banned the viewing of the World Cup. Crowds in Mogadishu gathered under trees and in iron-roofed huts to watch small TVs powered by gas generators before Islamic militias rode in and fired shots to disperse them. In protest, the residents set fire to piles of used tires, flooding the streets with a thick, choking smoke. Fighting would continue throughout the night as the Islamists moved to shut down cinemas and corner bars showing the matches.

And that night in Munich, where the beer gardens were alight with cheering, the streets were filled with honking cars and young men in scarves waving flags. The party would not stop until close to dawn. On my way home from the match I passed groups of young men sleeping huddled under their countries' flags on the cold floors of the train stations.

ROONEY AGONISTES

The next morning I dusted myself off and, on four hours of sleep, decided I would hit the trains to "nearby" Frankfurt, approximately 190 miles away, to catch England's first match.

And why not? One of the truly great moves of the German World Cup Organizing Committee was to give all of us in the press corps a free train pass to everywhere. So getting to Frankfurt seemed pretty easy, and we were still at the stage of the tournament when adrenaline staves off dizziness, blackouts, and other symptoms of the full-body punishment that is a World Cup.

After watching the morning news, which treated us to footage of a topless woman on Berlin's Strasse des 17. Juni, filmed by a group of enterprising pornographers who had taken advantage of the city's cleared streets (the producers—a pizza delivery driver and a bartender named Moe—said they "were new to the business" and "wanted to get some attention"), I staggered through the surprisingly tidy Viktualienmarkt (elves, I assume) and down the endless U-Bahn corridors to the train.

Frankfurt is an atypical city for Germany. It was once the seat for rulers of the Holy Roman Empire and today plays host to one of the world's largest stock exchanges. But because of the heavy bombing the city took during the Second World War, almost all of the old central city has been replaced with modern and Bauhaus buildings. This includes skyscrapers, which are rare on the Continent, giving Frankfurt the skyline of an American city.

Frankfurt is also home to the German Football Association (DFB) and a major hub of transportation for Germany—most people entering and exiting the country do so through the massive Frankfurt airport. As a result, the German World Cup organizing committee identified the city as one of the main bulwarks against hooligans. Prior to the Cup, fears had been heightened by incidents taking place in Germany's own leagues. Hansa Rostock fans had rioted in February, wounding at least eighteen policemen, and there were reports that German and Polish fans had brawled in the woods near the border in a prearranged skirmish the fall before. As a result, several thousand German troops were placed on call for the England vs. Paraguay game and the British police got into the act as well, sending uniformed and plainclothes officers to the Cup and using "banning orders" to keep troublesome fans from crossing the Channel. All told, some thirty thousand English fans were expected to hit the city, and at least a third of them were coming without tickets.

This is not unusual. When I arrived in Paris in May 2006 to see the World Cup's biggest competitor—the final of the Champions League—the city was swamped with thousands of English fans who had come without tickets or hotels. (Paris was to be a test-run, of sorts, for the new profiling methods meant to keep "Category C" hooligans away from the Cup games. It seemed to work, as there was little or no trouble.) In the streets, these fans crowded several deep around small TV screens in an attempt to see the big game in a drenching rain. One of the Irish bars in Pigalles was packed so tightly the crowd overflowed into the surrounding street, blocking traffic. The owners had set up a small TV outside, and pints were passed man to man overhead as fans sang, shoulder to shoulder.

After the game, for many finding a bed was as simple as finding an open doorway. A couple from the north of England bedded down in an ATM lobby with their watchdog to keep them company. Other fans made beelines for clubs, planning to spend the night drinking cheap beer, then catch early Eurostars back to England. Another set knew of an entrance to the Paris catacombs, where the walls in some places are made of human bones, and I watched as they disappeared through a crack in the wall into the dark. Having foolishly trusted a flaky (and short-lived) assistant to make my travel arrangements, I was myself *sans hotel,* and being of a more nervous disposition, stuck with five fans who made for the Saint-Lazare train station, where we slept out on the platform.

As I rolled into Frankfurt, the city was just waking up, bleary and bloated after Germany's opening-day win.

The mood on the streets was one of gaiety, or what passes for "gaiety" among English fans. This is perhaps not what the rest of us think of as a good time. In fact, most Americans would find partying English downright menacing.

The English like to drink: They make college girls on a Friday night look like amateurs. The last time I went out to drink with a group of my British colleagues, we began easy enough with pints and moved on to a good dozen bottles of wine. By the time I had tapped out, they had progressed to tumblers of scotch and were on their way out the door to a strip club in Soho. That night I lost a perfectly good pair of glasses, somehow bluffed R.E.M.'s Mike Mills into thinking I'd played with him at some point,* ran up an enormous bar tab that my employers weren't possibly going to pay, got in a traffic accident when the cab I was in rammed another cab, and ended up passing out fully clothed in a room that, thank god, I'd paid for. I wasn't really sure at the time I woke up, but, yes, yes, it was my room.

Now, imagine this sort of pub crawl in the glaring light of day, beginning as soon as one wakes up. In America we call this "alcoholism." In England they call it "getting ready for some footy." The vast majority of English fans aren't bad—they're knowledgeable about the game, passionate about good football, and even perfect gentlemen. And, yes, they're almost always men. The problem is, in every group, there are always one or two for whom alcohol leads directly to combustion and, in general, there is almost a calculated air of menace around England's fans. Few groups take the concept of football as war as seriously as they do, and there is no group whose rites and totems are as martial. Their terrace chants are deliberately provocative (they have been known to give the Nazi salute), and there is an unconcealed air of excitement over the prospect of things devolving into open confrontation or "going off." For the English, the bars and streets around an arena are places to occupy and conquer, and this is one reason they are widely and vehemently disliked. Once in a great while

*Actually, I had, sort of, but that's another story altogether.

their penchant for violence can be funny. At one point I saw two English louts take on an erratic Polish fan who had been singing, shirtless, in the street for a few hours while his companions dozed facedown at an outside table nearby. The English, understandably sick of his version of the Polish national anthem, confronted him as an easy mark and gave him a good shove. Rubber-legged, the Pole teetered over onto one leg, dropped his fist down near his ankle, and rebounded to sock one of the English fans dead on the jaw. As the English fan's head snapped back, it caught his pal's chin, sending him tumbling as well, and, suddenly, both were out cold on the cobblestones. The singer's friends glanced up briefly, decided he was okay, and put their heads back down on the table. The singer didn't miss a note.*

Still, though moments of levity like this are few and far between, in the hours before the England vs. Paraguay game, things were relatively calm. Touts who were asking six hundred euros for sixty-euro tickets were finding takers; beach balls were being boinked about the city center; and the English fans, draped in the traditional red and white of the St. George's Cross, were turning crimson, thanks to a prodigious consumption of lager and the cloudless day. Many fans gathered on the banks of the Main River to watch the game on the huge TV screens set up for the event; others traipsed around the local bars and beer gardens, crowding around whatever TVs could be found. And, most charmingly, small boys pranced about mimicking the "robot," a stiff-limbed '80s

---

*I made the mistake of busting out laughing at this, which resulted in my being roped in for a few shots of extremely strong Polish vodka and toasts to Poland before I could beg off and be on my way. Polish vodka tastes like grass. In fact, I think this stuff was made from grass.

craze and the celebratory dance of England forward Peter Crouch of Liverpool.

Crouch, a gangly man (he's six foot seven), walks with a perpetual hunch, as if he fears taking up any more airspace than he already does, but on the field he is an explosive pinwheel of limbs and sweat. He makes an atypical forward, given that his position requires quick bursts of speed and a relative economy of motion. And yet, somehow, Crouch is able to marshal an entirely ungainly package in the service of scoring.

Never a fan favorite, he was a late addition to the English squad and was greeted with howls of outrage. He was booed on the pitch by England's own supporters when he made an appearance in a pre–World Cup friendly against Poland. Things changed, however, when Crouch scored a superb goal against Hungary in another pre–World Cup warm-up and celebrated by performing the jerky dance that he later said he'd seen at a party at David Beckham's house (on TV; he wasn't invited). Overnight, he was a media sensation, and no longer the man who had been greeted with catcalls of "freak" at Anfield. Still, his new celebrity can't have felt very good: Here was a guy who'd been bounced around seven clubs in his career, and who had weathered an embarrassing nineteen-game streak at Liverpool without scoring, being celebrated not for succeeding but for acting silly.

But maybe that's what it took. The venom that had been tossed Crouch's way was never really about him. The fans disliked him simply because he wasn't the starter England was praying for. That man was the injured Wayne Rooney, of Manchester United, on whom the English had decided to pin their hopes.

———

Wayne Rooney grew up in Croxteth, a tough, bereft area out-side of Liverpool. As he was a poor student, soccer was about all Rooney had, and he was very good at it. A number of years ago I was in Liverpool to interview the American forward Brian McBride, who at the time was on loan from MLS to local club Everton. McBride, who is not one to throw bou-quets, told me about this sixteen-year-old kid in practice: "I've never seen anything like it; he puts every single shot on net," he said. That kid was Rooney. Rooney made a splash at Ever-ton and became one of the youngest players ever to appear in a Premier League match. A few years later Rooney would play for England in the 2004 European Championships, a some-what audacious move given his young age, and after a stellar run of form he would be hailed as the best English prospect in a generation. He was not yet twenty.

Called by some the "white Pelé," Rooney is a gritty, tough striker who plays with an abandon that is both thrilling and terrifying. He is as tough in practices as he is on game day, and his ferocity and speed have made him one of the most feared players in the world game.

However, Rooney is not without controversy. In 2002 threats were allegedly made by members of organized crime— newspaper reports fingered the Clerkenwell Syndicate, led by Terry Adams, who has been called one of the UK's biggest gangsters—against his agent, Paul Stretford, apparently in an effort to get control of the young star. The case went to trial, whereupon Stretford perjured himself on the stand in recount-ing how exactly he came to represent the footballer, and the case collapsed. And Rooney's ultralucrative book contract— a £5 million deal with HarperCollins for a multivolume auto-biography—has come under fire, not only for the hefty size of

the deal, but also because his former manager, Everton's David Moyes, has charged that parts of it are simply untrue.*
Rooney has also been libeled: He won a £100,000 judgment against two British tabloids that alleged he had assaulted his girlfriend, Coleen McLoughlin.

But the English press has covered his every move with a gimlet eye, not only because of his talent and these court cases but also because Rooney sums up something elemental in the English psyche.

Since the collapse of the British Empire, the country has been fighting against what might best be described as a collapse of self-esteem. The English tend to believe they are due credit for a great many things (including the language in which this book is written) and this has led to a well-satirized pomposity. Despite a good amount of self-awareness, however, it is hard for the English to escape a deep sense of loss, of expectations unfulfilled, and of status reduced.

The British welfare state—which Rooney, once a tenant of bleak council housing, benefited from—is enormous, and the nation's government is today best described as a sort of elected dictatorship, promising a macho central government that conceals the fact that the British place in the world has sharply declined, along with its economy. Furthermore, since the collapse of the empire, a great many former imperial subjects have come home to roost. England, which once viewed even Scotland and Ireland as "foreign," struggles today to serve a multiethnic population, and has some deep-seated racial

---

*Moyes has sued Rooney, HarperSport, and a newspaper, the *Daily Mail*, which excerpted parts of the book before it was published in September 2006. Incidentally, reviews of the book have not been kind.

problems as a result.* To England's credit, this struggle is open and publicly discussed, with little of the posturing that afflicts American politics. That doesn't change the fact that high taxes, a stagnant economy, a massive but fraying social safety net, and ethnic, religious, and racial tensions have made some segments of the population bitter—and deeply nostalgic for the glory days of empire, simplicity, and winning football.

Football has remained remarkably unchanged from its genesis over 150 years ago[†] as a game played by "Geordie" (or Northern English and Scottish) miners. Most sport was the pursuit of Europe's idle rich, largely concerned with individual achievement and self-betterment through athletics. To a member of the working class, this world was so far away as to be nonexistent. A factory worker with a family to support had no time for activities such as hunting or running—leisure activities for folks with lots of free time on their hands.[‡] Football was different. It was a workingman's game, a splinter of

---

*It must be said that England has handled this integration far better than other cultures and I doubt that when the American empire collapses the United States will handle it with the evenhandedness and openness the British have.

[†]I realize in saying this that "football" games have existed since the onset of recorded history. Early Chinese and Mayan and Aztec civilizations played ceremonial games involving feet and a single ball (or, as it were, a human head in the case of the South Americans and the early Picts of Scotland); and Renaissance Italy had a courtly game that gained popularity in Venice and resembled Hacky Sack. But the codified, club game of "association football," or "soccer," was a Scottish and English invention of the mid-to-late 1860s, and this is the game we refer to. It is also the one most people play and watch today.

[‡]That social divide is growing again today, and it may account for some of the fervor for the game in "new" areas such as Asia.

rugby that trickled down from the English universities to the back lots and fields of a newly industrial society. The shift to seeing sports as spectator entertainment began when the idle wealthy decided that, well, they'd rather be a bit more idle. In 1913, a time when class conflict was in flame not just in Europe but in America as well, soccer first bubbled up into mass consciousness as a spectator sport, and one associated with the working and middle classes.

For a few pence a workingman in London could stand at the Clock End of a stadium called Highbury in the northern end of the city in 1913 and watch Woolwich Arsenal play for the first—and last time—in the second division.* Previously, entertainment for the working classes had been the "blood sports" like cockfighting and boxing. Football was the first popular team sport, and it benefited from the fact that its players came not from the upper crust, but from the same factories and mines as the spectators. As a result, football teams put down deep roots in the communities they came from. Not only did local lads play for the home side, the team itself became a source of pride (or chagrin) for its community.

This was a pan-Western phenomenon. In Chicago, work teams—such as the now-long-defunct Manhattan Chicago—played soccer in the shadow of the meatpacking yards and the factories. In Italy and Mexico, sports clubs that once catered to what we call the Olympic events started to field soccer teams, sponsored by the very companies that supplied the players. In fact, some industrialists thought that if the men

---

*Arsenal is the only club in English history that has never been relegated from the top division.

were "distracted" with football, they'd be too tired to join the rabble-rousers or the Luddites.*

But another curious thing happened along the way—football teams and football grounds became sources of catharsis for a population that had few other avenues to vent their frustrations. The classic example of this transference is Glasgow Celtic, a club formed by Irish Catholic immigrants in Scotland that remains today a focus for religious tensions in the country.

Soccer as proxy conflict is a difficult concept for American sports fans to understand, and in the U.S. press the issue of soccer-related violence has rarely received the careful treatment it deserves.† The truth is that many American fans would feel genuinely threatened at big, important soccer matches between traditional rivals. And why not? The energy at Old Trafford for a Manchester United–Arsenal match is fed by a century of rivalry and class friction. While analogies have been made to some American teams—the Oakland Raiders, for example—they are false ones; American sports are almost purely spectator entertainment. World football matches are not—they are a proxy for conflict. Fact is, you're not *supposed* to feel comfortable at a Boca Juniors–River Plate game in Argentina.

The longevity of these teams has unfortunately allowed years of slights and conflicts to be stored up and reenacted today. Most of the teams playing today in England, Argentina,

---

*Unfortunately for them, this was not, and continues not to be, the case, as South Africa most recently discovered with the fall of apartheid. There, political opposition to the government was generated through black township football clubs.

†Traditionally, the American media only reports on the sport when something bad happens.

Italy, and Spain were formed at the turn of the twentieth century. Blackburn Rovers, a team in the English Premier League
(EPL) in 2006, won the first division in the 1911–12 and
1913–14 seasons; today's powerhouse Manchester United finished a lowly fourteenth. Highbury's tenant, Woolwich Arsenal, went on to drop the Woolwich in its name and gain
promotion to the first division.

Association football, or "soccer," was already about fifty
years old at this point. And with the formation of the English
Football Association, the sport caught fire with the public. As
a testament to its growing importance in the national consciousness, real waves were made in March of 1913 when
Holland beat England in soccer for the first time. It was "a
disaster," according to newspapers of the day—and perhaps
the first hint that Britain's dominance in the sport was waning.

The game of 1913 would be instantly recognizable to fans
today. While the technology was cruder—soccer balls were
made of tanned brown leather with laces and lumpy rectan-
gular bits that, when wet, turned the stuffing as hard as concrete—the basic idea was the same.* Today, players wear shin
guards and have expensive doctors, diet, and exercise regi-
mens; rayon has replaced wool as the jersey material of
choice; and balls are waterproof. But the skills needed to suc-

---

*In fact the 2-3-5 formation of players, credited with transforming the
game from a rough-and-tumble free-for-all into a skilled, touch-oriented
game, was pioneered by a club called Preston North End around this time.
What is a 2-3-5? Well, it's an arrangement of resources: Two players act as
defenders in front of a goalkeeper; three players form a midfield phalanx;
and five players, in a line from wing to wing, receive the ball and try to
score. For the purposes of this book I've tried to limit the jargon, but know
that when you hear a phrase such as "4-4-2," it refers to how players occupy
a field and the definition of their roles in the game.

ceed at the sport are the same as ever. It is probable that a top player of the 1950s would be just as potent a force today as he was then. What has changed, of course, is the expense—the game famously described as a "sport of gentlemen played by hooligans" is today a very big, and very global, business.

Now Highbury is gone. Players are no longer gathered from mills and factories but developed and traded in a world-wide bazaar. A decent player may earn £10,000* a week—an incredible sum in 1913—while stars earn many multiples of that. The scope of the game is also far greater: Today soccer is arguably the biggest financial enterprise in the sports world with cash flow in the trillions and outposts in every corner of the globe. Even Antarctica, a continent largely populated by American scientists and their support crew, has a team de-spite a year-round average temperature of −60°F.

Soccer purists and nostalgists alike yearn for the days when football teams were made up of local neighborhood lads, the kind of men one could sit and have a drink with after the match. Journalists and fans both gripe about the new gen-eration of celebrity footballers and sniff at their expensive spouses, corporate handling, and seemingly unrestrained egos. And yet football is more popular than it ever has been. Despite all this money, the game—and the Cup itself—remain a cher-ished possession of the working class and poor worldwide. While the Cup is so large that staging it today requires the steerage of the moneyed classes, its most fervent support comes from the same ranks that the player base does: the poor. My colleague Francis Holoway, who works as part of the med-ical staff with River Plate, ruefully observed that while their

---

*$20,000 at the current rate of exchange.

American counterparts undoubtedly have more balanced lives, "the fact is poverty creates desire, which creates better football."

The ethics of football, especially that the world's richest sport seems to require a vast contingent of very poor people to provide both its players and its fans, remain troubling. And yet despite the obvious conflicts—the fact that most major teams are now either owned by fabulously wealthy men or are controlled by large investment funds—the myth of football as a "classless" game remains. Although ticket prices are exorbitant in England's Premiership—from £30 ($60) tickets per match at middling grounds to the extreme of the new Diamond club seating area at Arsenal's Emirates Stadium, which requires an annual fee of £22,500 ($45,000) just to get in the door— football remains in popular thought the "people's game." And, despite the fact that the game is moving farther and farther away from its deeply proletarian roots, the same working-class men and women who form the core of soccer's faithful are spending more time and money on it than ever before.

Oddly enough, those high ticket prices were originally instilled to keep those very "people" out. England, which suffered a terrible problem with soccer-related violence in the 1970s and 1980s, raised admission in an attempt to attract a "higher class of fan." Now the "real" fans—the ones so often spotlighted on TV, the banner-waving, flare-burning rabble— have largely been confined, like animals in a zoo, to far corners of the grounds. (Nowhere is this more evident than in Italy, where the "ultras," the most rabid, fanatical supporters, are often let in free by management. There they unwittingly serve as entertainment for their bourgeois neighbors, who are keen to have a taste of the danger of football without any of the ramifications.)

Not all of this is a bad thing: In the 1970s Chelsea's Stamford Bridge was a virtual no-go zone, and Highbury was home to a notorious group of "casuals."* "Colors"—scarves, shirts, anything orange in the case of Dundee United on match days—were banned from public places. I was once ejected from the Wellgate Shopping Centre (a low-lying mall that happened to be a convenient cut-through from the train station to Tannadice) in Dundee for wearing a United scarf on a match day, for fear that I would incite violence. I was seven or eight at the time, which either shows you how seriously people took this or the absurd lengths to which fans were persecuted. And there is no question that the atmosphere at the games was dangerous, fueled by religion and tribal conflict and, of course, alcohol.

At Stamford Bridge, I once saw Chelsea play Arsenal. I stood on the terraces, a tiny head popping up, trying to see over the big, tough lads in front of me. To this day, to avoid trouble, visiting fans are segregated physically from home fans. (If you look closely at a European club match on TV, you'll see barbed wire strung between the segments of the stands, and sometimes even a "moat," a large ditch between the stands and the pitch in which police officers wait to nab rowdy fans.) So, standing at the Arsenal end on that day, we waited an hour while the London police escorted the Chelsea fans out of the park and to the Underground. Unfortunately, the Underground

---

*"Casuals" was the generic nickname for hooligan groups; they dressed not in fan colors but casual clothing, which in that era was rather snappy. Some of them displayed mordant wit alongside their violence: My older cousin, Duncan Murray, was once beaten up outside Pittodrie by Aberdeen's fans, who graciously left him a business card after the job was done. The card read: "You have been serviced by the Aberdeen Casuals."

had broken down, and when our turn came to be marched like prisoners down a large cordon patrolled by bobbies on horses, and patrolmen with large dogs on leashes, the two groups of fans met in the stairwell and on the platform of the track.

I remember a police officer grabbing me by my collar and pinning me against a wall for my own safety. The fans brawled in front of me in a scrum, and the platform became slick with blood. The police let the dogs off their leashes, and they leaped into the pack, hauling men out by their arms and throats. A subway car pulled up and the police began throwing people on board, packing them in so tightly no one could move. As the car pulled out, I watched the dogs licking the blood off the concrete and playing with the scraps of clothing left behind. The faces of the men, pressed against the glass of the car, slowly moved to my left and into the tunnel. They were flushed, starving for air, and desperate. Ten minutes later, a train pulled into the empty station, and life returned to normal.

Today the Premier League's grounds are undoubtedly less threatening than they once were. There are no standing-room sections (the "terraces"), which were magnets for violence and gang activity. Women and children now attend matches without fear. For younger fans, used to luxury stadiums or high TV production values, the old bare-bones pitches are lost forever.

To those nostalgic for the past, Rooney is seen as being the epitome of the working-class footballer and a certain classic "Englishness": He is envisioned as tough, self-sufficient, and fair-minded,* with a lovely girlfriend. In reality he is

---

*Interestingly, these same traits are often ascribed to Chaucer, the most English of poets, and his *Canterbury Tales*. This is not a throwaway point. Read on.

thuggish, poorly educated, and somewhat thick. He has been dismissed several times in high-profile matches after his temper got the better of him and has been involved in on- and off-field rows, most notably with England's then captain David Beckham and Blackburn's Michael Gray. His fiancée, the gaudy Coleen McLoughlin, is best known for her propensity for giddy, expensive shopping sprees. Rooney is like a great many other English soccer players (and, to be fair, American athletes) and is almost iconic for a poor subset of the English working class, the "chavs."

The word *chav* is of uncertain etymology. Some claim it is an acronym, for "cheap and vulgar" or "council housed and violent"; either definition fits. It describes a subset of working-class English that should be familiar to anyone who has lived among urban American poor: a flamboyantly materialistic group that believes a grim setting can be escaped via expensive clothing and jewelry. The chavs closely resemble American hip-hop culture; in the States they would be called "white trash" or "wiggers." *Chav* is not a term of endearment.

Unsurprisingly, while the elegant Beckham came to represent English football with his "metrosexual" look, Rooney's belligerence and straightforward, head-down style of play is more appealing to many Englishmen of a certain class. In their eyes, Rooney is a tough, sure, but he never gives up or rolls around faking an injury. Whereas Beckham is a remote tabloid figure, Rooney, despite being handsomely paid, is "one of the lads"—and an English lad in the way that a David Beckham, a Peter Crouch, or a Michael Owen never really can be. Beckham is seen as posh and overpaid; Crouch is a figure of comedy; and Owen, despite easily being the best technical player on the team, doesn't play in the "English style." This perhaps accounts for Rooney's cross-cultural appeal. A Catholic in an overwhelmingly Protestant and Anglican country, he is far more likely to be disliked for leaving Everton for Manchester United than for his religion. That alone marks a sea change from years past.

Rooney was, therefore, one of the most important players entering the 2006 World Cup—important to England in the way Fabio Cannavaro of Italy and Zinedine Zidane of France were to their teams, as embodiments of what fans think a national player should be. In the 2004 European Championships, Rooney had terrorized the opposition in group play, scoring four goals, but suffered an injury early in England's quarterfinal tie with host team Portugal. England would go on to lose that match on kicks, with Beckham missing a critical penalty attempt. The lesson learned there was: With Rooney in the lineup, England is unbeatable; without him, England is ordinary. Coming into the World Cup, then, fans and players alike relied on Rooney to provide a sort of center for the team.

The English are historically slow starters, having won only four matches in eleven World Cup openers prior to 2006, and in Frankfurt Rooney was not scheduled to play. The afternoon was a tense affair. England played true to form against Paraguay, a mid-level South American team that clawed its way into the Cup by virtue of surviving the Continent's unending qualification process.

The only goal of the match came three minutes in, when a free kick served from the left by Beckham ricocheted off the head of Paraguay's Carlos Gamarra and into the back of the net. After settling back, the England eleven hardly looked like convincing contenders for the title, with Frank Lampard failing to convert any remaining chances and the Paraguayans—

notably Nelson Valdes—gaining confidence as it dawned on them that the English were unable to put the sword to them. Most observers felt this was a soggy display—and laughter was heard from the international press corps when Beckham blamed the team's sluggishness on the "searing heat." It was actually 68° out, with a peak of 86° on the field in the direct sun.

Elsewhere, in Dortmund, the Swedes labored to a nil–nil draw with tiny Trinidad and Tobago, a result that sent the Caribbeans into gleeful celebration and the Swedes into dissension; star Freddie Ljungberg would sock a teammate at practice the next day. In Hamburg, Argentina gutted out a win against the Elephants of the Ivory Coast, a talented but untested side that relied heavily on the striker Didier Drogba of Chelsea. England–Paraguay was the worst game of the day.

Now, here's the great irony: Frankfurt was quiet. It was England that exploded.

More than two hundred people rioted in London during an open-air telecast of the game near Canary Wharf. The city of Liverpool was hit by fan violence as well, causing the government to pull the telecasts from viewing areas as bottles, chairs, and fists flew. The English press had a field day, flagellating the coach, the team, and themselves for the displays. The mood around the team was grim. For the next few days, the English players and their fans would be making heavy weather of things, while elsewhere in Germany the other English actors began to take the stage.

We're talking about, of course, the players' wives and girlfriends.

The "WAGs," as they became known, were followed by the press with the same breathless mania as are pop stars. Symptomatic of the need to have all-encompassing coverage of the national team, members of the media basically stalked them, detailing their shopping, spending, and "Baden-Baden" behavior. Between reports of the photographers literally falling over themselves for action shots and the women drunkenly stumbling about, the coverage became a carnival.

Did I mention that the English Football Association made the incredible gaffe of putting the WAGs at the same hotel it had billeted the journos? Yes. This gave a resentful press* acres of material to work with, everything from Frank Lampard's girlfriend dancing on a table to "I Will Survive" at one A.M. to the WAGs' daily assault on the shops. According to the press, shopping and sleeping off the night before dominated the group's activity calendar, and the tabloids conscientiously reported each purchase made: Ms. McLoughlin was said to have spent $1,700 in ten minutes one day, a splurge topped by a $10,000 traipse through one boutique by the WAGs en masse. Much ink was spilled over whether not-quite WAG (and not at all rich) Melanie Slade, the seventeen-year-old girlfriend of seventeen-year-old Theo Walcott, was fitting in with this gang, and much was made of the ladies' food and liquor bill. At one point the English Football Association took time out to reassure all of Britain that the women were paying their own way.

The WAGs were a gift for the weary press, and they set off some great volleys in both countries. When the German tabloid *Bild* labeled Beckham's sister "fat," the *Sun* parried the next day with a shot of his wife, Victoria, with the headline THE BEAUT, next to a dumpy German barmaid labeled "Das

---

*The average reporter on the English team junket was required to pony up about £17,000 ($34,000), not including meals, transportation, or "extras." As you can imagine, sticker shock whetted the appetite of the vulpine U.K. media. For comparison, two Americans at the Cup spent under $25,000, total.

Boot." Cleverer papers, which sensed that the English team would not live up to its billing, ran stories about the stamina of the wives at bars and shops, noting that if only their lads had the same reserves, they'd be unbeatable on the pitch.

One could argue that the British press was trying to make the World Cup gender-equitable, giving their female readers subjects they were interested in, but that would be bullshit. In reality, this was a mean-spirited snipefest, with penurious reporters savaging well-heeled women. The *Daily Mail*'s Stephen Glover was particularly appalled by these women, harrumphing in a famously over-the-top column* (that also took on Rooney, Nike ads, the Church, Norse mythology, and the kitchen sink) that this trash with cash was a threat to the empire. Bizarrely, Glover's real problem seemed to be that they were there at all and that the English side was not preparing in monastic isolation. In the event, England, with or without the still-injured Rooney, was so disappointing that some of the best, funniest, and meanest English reporting at the World Cup came not about the team but at the expense of this collection of pretty, lower-class, and often poorly educated ladies. What would the Wife of Bath say?

Rooney would return for the next match, a 2–0 win against Trinidad and Tobago on June 15. But in the interim, the other teams were getting ready to go on stage.

---

*Entitled DID ROONEY REALLY NEED TO POSE FOR THIS REVOLTING PICTURE?, it ran in the *Daily Mail* on June 21, 2006. It should be noted that best thing to come out of the WAGs was Marina Hyde's sharp and funny "diary," supposedly penned by Sven-Göran Eriksson's girlfriend, Nancy Dell'Olio, that ran intermittently in the *Guardian*. Hyde, a columnist, at least gave Dell'Olio the dignity of being clever, even if most of her antics revolved around alcohol and men.

5

THE BIG MONEY

I got back to Munich late after the England vs. Paraguay game. I was tired, in that half-awake, half-not state you get in after spending a week on trains and in smoky press rooms, living off sausage sandwiches and a peculiar, leafy, paste-colored vegetable. I never discovered the origin of this tasteless treat, but I think it was a cabbage derivative. The shutters in the train station were closed, and even the newsagent hadn't gotten around to unwrapping his bales. I nicked a copy of the *Guardian,* leaving a few euros on the stack, and walked up the flights of stairs to the dawn. I passed a group of snoring fans using the St. George's Cross as their blanket as I made for the Marienplatz.

The sun was just coming up over the old town hall. I turned the corner and cut through the Viktualienmarkt, where two old ladies were drinking their liters of morning beer. Mike, the bartender, waved to me. I'd become a familiar sight as there weren't many people with full sleeves of tattoos in Munich (or at least few who got up in the daytime).

I took the shortcut to my flat through a dingy little alley; the brothel, serviced by Vietnamese and Laotian prostitutes, was just ahead, but it was far too early for the girls to be open for business. I'd see them around noon, out for one of those repellent mackerel sandwiches, flirting with the cashier, perhaps drumming up a little business for later. (It seemed to be a crappy Cup for the sex trade. The hookers I talked to were bored out of their minds and actually saw their wages fall.) The girls always seemed to be wearing the same outfits, or variants thereof, and I'd later be told the women had arrived to work on their backs with just the clothing they were wearing. They hung their washed-out underwear up to dry in the alley behind the buildings, and if you went to the top of the church and knew where to look, you could see them, gamely wringing out laundry each afternoon.

Absentmindedly, I kicked a can along the alley, a bad habit I picked up in New York. When it hit with a clunk instead of a clank, I realized it was actually a small glass jar, the kind used for baby food; the label had a big picture of a pineapple. I picked it up, meaning to throw it in a recycling bin. Then I noticed another jar sitting on the window ledge of the smoky bar that always seemed to have open-wheel racing on the TV. When I walked back toward it, I saw another, then another, down the alley toward the street.

Curious, I followed this trail of jars. I found a cardboard flat they had once been in, another jar in the street, and another few under the portico of the town hall. The trail went down the stairs and back into the U-Bahn. I looked again at the jar—who would be eating baby food? But the contents weren't pureed—whole rings of pineapple had been stuffed into these tiny glass jars.

Now I was confused. How did they get big rings of pineapple into these tiny jars? I stood there for a few minutes, turning the jar over in my hand, looking at the tiny jar mouth and wondering what kind of mutant pineapple ring might fit inside it. Was it one big ring? A succession of tiny rings? Were the rings cut very thin? I walked down the stairs and followed the trail of jars . . . right to the English fans knocked out under their flag. They were surrounded by half-eaten pineapple and tiny glass jars. One of them still had syrup all over his beard.

By this time, the newsagent had arrived and we looked at each other, then back at the English.

"Drunks," he said, in English, and started ripping open his bales.

I went home, to get up four hours later.

The Cup didn't begin in poorer Eastern Germany until June 11, when Leipzig hosted Holland against another former Soviet bloc nation, the then twinned Serbia and Montenegro. The mood in Leipzig was markedly different from anywhere I'd been—or would be until the finals—in West Germany. The fans were happy, right enough, and the younger people I met were charming, but the population as a whole was wary, as it had been during the draw. When I mentioned this in passing to some of my colleagues, I was told it was just an "inborn 'Ossi' unfriendliness."

Later I would decide the emotion I felt from the East Germans was not hostility but loss. Fifteen years after the collapse of the state, there remained a palpable mourning, whether for the safety net of the socialist state or, more commonly, for something very fundamental that had long ago been forcibly removed, namely privacy and the freedom to be left alone.

The perfection of the East German surveillance state the Lipsi* had grown up in was rivaled only by present-day North Korea; in efficiency, the GDR spying might even have surpassed that of Pyongyang. While there was one Gestapo officer for every 2,000 citizens during the Third Reich, and the Soviets assigned one KGB officer for every 5,830 persons under Stalin, in the GDR, one Stasi was responsible for every 63 people. And, if the documents uncovered after reconciliation can be believed, that ratio, given informants, might actually have approached one for every 6.5 people. During the existence of the GDR, the residents knew they were being spied on—they assumed it was 1 in 50. But 1 in 7?

The Stasi were no slackers. In 1985 they planned an invasion of Western Berlin (that the West, apparently, was unaware of), and if this transpired or if the GDR fell into crisis, any crisis, the secret police were supposed to open envelopes from Berlin labeled "Day X" and proceed to arrest 420 people an hour—for a total of 89,939 people. Each arrestee was supposed to pack for detention, using a list that went right down to clean underwear and a toothbrush. In fact, instead of carrying out their orders when "Day X" came in 1989, the Stasi locked themselves in their bunkers.

If it is difficult to wrap your mind around the idea that people being arrested would quietly pack for their detention, consider that in 1989, when Leipzigers finally stormed the Runden Ecke and deposed the Stasi, the crowd was halted at

---

*A common nickname for the Leipzigers, and also a name for a very funny and peculiar dance described in Anna Funder's brilliant and horrifying *Stasiland* (Granta Books, 2004). I am indebted to Ms. Funder for the figures in this paragraph.

the front door by officers asking to see identity cards. The protesters automatically produced them. Then, without a fuss, they took the building. Even a GDR coup had rules.

In Berlin's Stasimuseum you can see footage of the citizens taking that building, walking by evidence of how their masters lived. Predictably, while the population skimped, the Stasi had been surviving fairly well, with a barbershop, a luxurious supermarket, and rooms filled with documents on its own people collected from all across the country. The faces of the Berliners in this film are not what you might expect— these are not the people who danced on the Wall, singing and screaming in sheer joy. These people look tired and disgusted.

The people in Leipzig looked pretty tired and disgusted, too, when I was there. One of the weird things about a Cup intended to promote a reunified Germany was that Leipzig was the only host city in the former East. The reasoning was that there were no facilities, but that was not entirely true: What was lacking was money to fix up stadiums. The region had been ruined twice, by World War II and immediately again by the Red Army, who upon taking the region sent a great deal of heavy industry and valuables back to Moscow under the rubric of solidarity and brotherhood. Now, in the run-up to the Cup, many Western commentators bemoaned the sums spent fixing up the East as money going down a rabbit hole.

Add to this the dire pretournament warnings about going East. A number of wire services carried grim predictions of Polish hooligans streaming over under cover of darkness and of neo-Nazi activity.

Finally, the Cup was a triumph of commercialism ideologically opposed to what Easterners had been taught for forty years. The Fan Fests and the billboards hawked not only

Western-made items but capitalism itself. It seems to me now that Germany's Cup organizers made a conscious decision to leave the Ossis out; the Germany that was on show was the diligent, capitalist West, not the "backward," poorer East. No wonder not all Ossis were enthusiastic.

But not just Ossis were being left out. Getting into the games was proving difficult for the average fan. One in six tickets went to Cup sponsors such as Budweiser or Hyundai. A further one in nine, despite being counted in the general sale pool, went to "hospitality," or corporations and the extremely wealthy. According to FIFA, of the 3.07 million tickets available, 1 million went right off the bat to sponsors, hospitality, and global TV. Another 276,000 went to German fans via their Football Association, and roughly 20 percent of seats went to folks like yours truly, a member of the international media. All in all, the chance of a fan getting in to see his team was remarkably low: A credible estimate was that only 8 percent of tickets in the stadium went at face value directly to a fan.

So, scalping—which FIFA had strenuously tried to curtail with all sorts of rigmarole, such as putting people's names on their tickets and trying to check IDs in the giant crowds— was omnipresent. FIFA officials got in on the act, too, a common but unrecognized practice. FIFA was extremely embarrassed when one of its officials had the poor form to be caught: Botswana's Ismail Bhamjee had the book thrown at him and was sent home from the Cup after confessing to selling tickets for the England vs. Trinidad game for two hundred euros above face value. Cynics wondered how he'd managed to get so little: Tickets to that game were going for as much as two thousand euros.

So where did the average fan, priced out of the arenas, go? To the Fan Fest, a sprawling celebration held in each of the twelve host cities. This was one area in which organizers failed, grossly underestimating fan interest. In Munich, organizers expecting at most ten thousand fans were shocked when ten times that number arrived. Police were forced to deny fans entry to viewing areas and to shut down the U-Bahn and S-Bahn trains heading out to where the Fan Fest was held. It was easy to see why the Fests were wildly popular. First, they were free, and generally packed with young people eager to see the games on one of the giant TV screens that were set up. Second, they were essentially outdoor malls, with a food court, beer tents, and licensed merch all readily available—though the water cost more than the beer. It was a bit like being at a tailgate, albeit one held at Great America.

The mood at most of these Fests was cheerful and inebriated. Early in the tournament, at a shockingly early hour, a huge straw hat about five feet wide, with TIJUANA scrawled on it in lime green letters, lurched dangerously close to my left eye. The brim flopped up to reveal a small, rather drunk fellow clutching a bottle of . . . well, something. "*SI SE PUEDE!*" screamed the wearer, with halitosis that could sterilize a frog at ten yards. He cheerfully offered the bottle to me, making the universal motion for "drink up." I declined, and he stumbled back into the crowd.

The Fan Fests required an Olympian endurance for such fraternal behavior; every day tens of thousands came, drank, cleaned out the merch tents, and staggered back to the S-Bahns from whence they came. In 2002 the Fan Fests were debuted in order to solve a very real problem (called the Sea of Japan) that separated the countries hosting the tournament. Here, however, they were supposedly democratizing the overpriced Cup, and there's no doubt people enjoyed them—and the Germans made a buck.

But the Fan Fests changed something essential about the World Cup, moving it away from being the world's greatest sporting event and toward being only a party. Other sporting events have galas surrounding them—the Super Bowl is notorious for its run-up week—but what few people talked about was that the Fan Fests were yet another way to separate the actual fans from the event they were attending. While the corporate sponsors got the seats at the arenas—and those they didn't use were sold off to fans at huge markups—the trend of segregating the working-class lifeblood of the game, and diluting its real passion, continued, all in the pursuit of cash.

But back to Leipzig, for one of the first-round games true fans would be able to attend. Zentralstadion greeted the teams with bright sunlight and an overwhelmingly pro-Dutch crowd, dressed head to toe in orange: orange sunglasses, orange hats, orange face paint, orange shirts, orange socks, orange lederhosen, and, among the exhibitionists, even a few orange bra-and-panty sets.

The crowd was raucous. A loose rendition of the triumphal march from *Aïda* echoed as Holland's coach, the scrawny, sunburned Marco van Basten, set to pacing on the sideline. A gangly man, van Basten looks like a child who has grown out of his clothes and whose mother has neglected to buy him a new set, but he was a fashion plate compared to Serbia's Ilija Petković, whose unrelentingly grim manner foreshadowed his team's path.

Historic hatreds, street violence, a grim past, and superb athletes: The Serbia and Montenegro team brought them all to the table. The former territories of Yugoslavia—which were occupied by the Nazis, suffered partisan warfare and dictatorship, then unraveled after the death of Marshal Tito—remain wrecked after the most recent partition and civil war. Serbia and Montenegro have tremendous problems with unemployment and alcoholism, as well as a particularly vicious organized crime syndicate that specializes in human trafficking, oil- and gunrunning, and narcotics. From a soccer standpoint, however, the region remains remarkable: Yugoslavia was such a rich fount of talent that all of its former republics are competitive in the European theater. Serbia and Montenegro qualified for the Cup when it beat bitter Balkan rivals Bosnia and Herzegovina 1–0 on a seventh-minute goal from Mateja Kezman on October 12, 2005, in Sarajevo.

Predictably, that all-Balkan game—only the third match between the two former Yugoslav republics since the 1992–95 civil war that left two hundred fifty thousand dead in Bosnia—was serious business. One fan reportedly lost a finger, another suffered a fractured nose; in total six fans were seriously injured as violence flared throughout the crowd of fifty-five thousand. Afterward, while celebrating Serbia and Montenegro's victory, Bosnian Serbs—who don't consider Bosnia their homeland—burned flags and fought with police. Police reports estimated that ten thousand Serbian fans celebrated in Banja Luka, the capital of the Serb half of Bosnia, and the cops spent the day trying to prevent the crowd from smashing the windows of Muslim-owned stores. Eleven fans were "detained."

Unfortunately for the Serbia and Montenegro team, the

latest source of conflict came just prior to the tournament, when Serbia and Montenegro officially split their union; this would be the last time the country fielded a "unified" team. Sadly, the Serbs were quick—after all was said and done—to blame the team's performance on an overabundance of Montenegrin players.

But even without these new tensions, the Serbia and Montenegro team was hardly favored on the day. It came into the match having conceded only one goal in ten qualifying matches; it had gone unbeaten (one of only eight European sides to do so), winning six matches while drawing four. It looked very solid in the back and could be potent on counters, with the mercurial Kezman driving its attack. However, the Netherlands is one of the greatest teams in soccer history never to have won a World Cup. Seven-time finalists, the Dutch contribute players to leagues across the globe, have a well-respected top league (the Casino Eredivisie), and have inspired a system of play that is copied across the planet.

Called "total football," the system essentially requires all ten field players to be comfortable in any position. Players overlap and fall back as needed—preferably at blistering speed—to keep constant pressure on the opposition. Developed by Ajax coach Rinus Michels, who memorably used it to see off Inter Milan in the 1972 European Cup, total football is a dizzying style that is both individually demanding and highly tactical.

In American terms, total football is the equivalent of basketball's triangle offense; just as it took Michael Jordan to bring that system to perfection in the 1990s with the Chicago Bulls, the total football system saw its apogee in the 1970s with Dutch legend Johan Cruyff, who ran what fans called the

"Clockwork Orange."* The Dutch were runners-up in the Cup twice with this system, in 1974 and 1978.

Perhaps the epitome of this style is the well-remembered meeting between Argentina and Holland in the second round of the 1974 World Cup. Before the game, some neutrals thought the Argentines were a legitimate threat to favored Brazil. But playing in Gelsenkirschen, the South Americans were comprehensively whipped, with Cruyff setting the tone by netting a spectacular goal in the tenth minute on a five-pass play from midfield that concluded with Cruyff scissor-kicking the ball past a stunned Daniel Carnevali. The game would end 4–0 with Cruyff adding insult to injury in the ninetieth minute.

So Serbia and Montenegro was up against a tough opponent, and further, one that had their number. Even the former Yugoslavia hadn't been able to win against Holland in modern times and had been crushed at Euro 2000 in Rotterdam, in their last competitive meeting, when the Dutch cruised to a 6–1 win. With great creative players such as Arjen Robben and Ruud van Nistelrooy in Leipzig, the Dutch were favorites to make it out of one of the most difficult groups in the Cup.

The Serbs and the Dutch did have one thing in common, however: wretched fans. Oddly, for people considered among the most tolerant in the world, Dutch supporters are almost as loathed as England's. That's darn tough to accomplish. In later rounds some trouble would flare up, but despite the air of menace around both sets of fans as they entered Leipzig's arena, the day would be calm though the game was a tense one. It only took eighteen minutes for Serbia and Montene-

---

*Of course, most of the fans had not read Anthony Burgess's dystopian novel about juvenile delinquents and mind control.

gro's *Plavi* defense to collapse and Robben to score the only goal of the match. Playing the offside trap,* Serbia and Montenegro was caught out when Robin van Persie's cross from

---

*The concept of "offside" is somewhat like the infield fly rule in baseball: Once you understand it, it is a model of simplicity and common sense; sadly, getting to that serene state is a bit like solving an algebraic expression given only one factor. In a nutshell, a player is offside (and for the record, it is *not* "offsides," despite what people on TV tell you) when he attempts to receive the ball without having at least two opposing players between him and the goal line. And yes, I know that is well nigh incomprehensible; the officialese in FIFA's rule book is no better: "A player is offside if he is nearer to his opponents' goal line than both the ball and the second-to-last opponent." And, oh, by the way, "nearer to his opponents' goal line" means: "any part of his head, body, or feet is nearer to his opponents' goal line than both the ball and the second-to-last opponent. The arms are not included in this definition." Gripping stuff, huh?

Here's the deal: Basically, it's illegal to hang around near the goal with only the keeper to beat. In basketball, of course, this is perfectly legal— guards routinely heave the ball down the court for an easy, uncontested layup. But in soccer, if you could just sit around the goal, your colleagues could punt the ball down to you and you could go one-on-one with the keeper all day long. Cynics might say that would encourage scoring in this notoriously parsimonious sport, but the point is this behavior is deeply unsporting, and, as such, the concept of offside has existed since the very early days of the game. Thus, in practice, the rule requires that there be two players—a defender, a forward, anyone along with, presumably, the goalkeeper—between you and the goal line before you get the ball.

The "offside trap" was developed by teams as a defensive measure against swift forwards. What the defenders do is line up three or four abreast, and step up before the ball is served to put the forward in, *ta da*, an offside position. That's why you will see forwards hanging close to their defending man while looking back for the pass, only to suddenly streak away toward the goal in an effort to beat this trap, because for it to work, the defenders have to fight the impulse to step back after them.

The trap is a perilous thing to run nowadays because it depends on the judgment of the linesman, who is always supposed to be lined up with the last defender but who, in practice, frequently blows the call. Watch a few high-level games and you'll inevitably see a man called offside who actually wasn't, as well as a man called onside who was actually off. As a result, the trap is never run close to their own goal by smart teams.

the other half found Robben with space. Robben dribbled nearly thirty-five yards into the box to put a low, left-footed shot past keeper Dragoslav Jevrić. The crowd exploded—the orange-clad fans leaping out of their seats, screaming and applauding, as the white-clad Serbian fans sunk, glumly, as deeply as they could into the hard plastic chairs. Robben roared and ran across the face of the goal toward the crowd, pumping his arms in triumph like a weight lifter doing curls.

Jevrić would be tested by Robben repeatedly, making a diving save just three minutes later, and would have to watch the Chelsea winger all afternoon. Kezman and teammate Ognjen Koroman tried to tie things up for Serbia and Montenegro, the latter with a late foray in the first half from the edge of the box that had keeper Edwin van der Saar beat, but missed wide.

Serbia and Montenegro vs. Holland was one of the better games of an otherwise torpid first round, but the match would be most memorable, sadly, because of a sponsorship flap. An enterprising Dutch brewery, Grossbrauerei, had given Dutch fans a pair of orange lederhosen-style shorts with the purchase of any twelve-pack in Holland. Unlike the deliberately provocative orange German army helmets, the lederhosen were a gentle joke, innocent fun with Bavarian culture, and the truth is everyone liked them; the Munich barkeep near my flat asked if he could have my pair. They were sent to me along with a number of other charming Dutch trinkets commemorating the World Cup, including the "Wuppie," a madly popular orange, fuzzy, Ping-Pong-ball-sized creature given away at supermarkets. The "big Wuppie," the most prized item, was obtained by spending an ungodly amount of money on groceries and created such a craze that people were breaking into cars and stealing them. Heineken, which is the official sponsor of the Dutch team, gave away the orange sunglasses. But the Grossbrauerei lederhosen were viewed dimly by FIFA as a sort of guerrilla marketing tactic, even though it was hard to make out the brewery's logo unless you were in the stands.

At the Cup in South Korea, nonsponsor Nike had employed guerrilla marketing brilliantly, doing a far better job at getting its name out than official sponsor Adidas. Mindful of this setback to the sponsorship cash stream, FIFA was so concerned about marketing and naming rights in Germany that before the tournament it stripped every stadium of nonsponsor logos—even making Munich's Allianz Arena take down its sign, remember.* Heineken was apparently so miffed that folks showed up wearing rival gear to a pre-Cup friendly with Cameroon that officials forced spectators to take off the lederhosen and throw them away before entering the stadium. Grossbrauerei actually won a court decision in Holland forestalling such high-handed tactics in the future, but money talks, and when Dutch fans showed up in Stuttgart on June 16 for Holland's next game, against the Ivory Coast, they were greeted by burly security personnel who forced anyone wearing the orange shorts to take them off. Dumpsters outside the grounds were filled with orange cotton pants, and a lot of Dutch fans watched that game in their underwear.

The great lederhosen confrontation would be but the first

---

*This is hardly new: "Cleaning" stadiums has been standard protocol for the World Cup and many other big sporting events for decades. That doesn't make it any less silly: In the run-up to 2002, FIFA's operations people actually held a discussion about whether photographers should be asked to remove any personal clothing items branded with Nikon and Kodak logos or nomenclature! (This item was tabled.)

salvo in the corporate tournament's battle with spontaneity. Even Brazil's famously buoyant fans, who often come armed with instruments and drums, were only grudgingly allowed to bring their music into the stadium after long discussions with the German World Cup organizing committee and FIFA. It was finally decided that these fans would be allowed to play, seeing as that activity is one of the most magnetic things about a soccer match . . . but only if they stopped for the various advertisements and "infotainments" piped in over the PA. Wolfgang Niersbach, the vice president of the local Cup organizers, admitted to reporters that such a restriction probably killed the mood, but what could be done? The air time had been bought and paid for.

Meanwhile, the tension around Team USA had continued right up to its first match, on June 12 in Gelsenkirchen. Before the game, American and Czech fans mingled and partied together. Coca-Cola had parked a truck with a full sound system near one of the stadium entrances, and Czech fans sang along to Lynyrd Skynyrd's "Sweet Home Alabama." Who knew the Velvet Revolution had such Southern flair? Out at the Munich Fan Fest, though, some of the American fans seemed a bit clueless about exactly what they were going to see. One leaned over to me and said eagerly, "Hey, the USA is about to play Croatia."

The team would prove to be just as clueless. The television cameras caught the Americans as they walked into the bright sunlight of the stadium: They lined up for the anthem looking as though they were going to shit their pants. There really is no other way to describe it. The Czechs looked calm and determined; some were loosening their necks while others looked straight ahead, already in that concentrated quiet that blocks out the noise, the stadium, the spectators, and the cameras. The Czechs were *ready*. In contrast, the Americans looked jumpy and stunned: Pablo Mastroeni was covered in sweat, Oguchi Onyewu looked close to tears, and even the normally unflappable Keller was bouncing on the balls of his feet. Many were glancing around, mouthing the words to the anthem and fidgeting uncomfortably. The last time I had seen that kind of fear in a team's eyes was in 1998, when the USA lined up for its first match against Germany in France, at the Parc des Princes. The players had just realized what it felt like to walk into a full stadium and play a game the entire world would be watching.

One of the great mysteries of soccer is why the world's largest consumer of sports has never had much use for the beautiful game. American professional sports look at soccer with a mixture of awe and fear. Why? Soccer in the United States is overwhelmingly a participant phenomenon, and it is gobbling up grassroots participants from other sports at an alarming rate. Across the nation, football and baseball fields are being plowed under to make room for yet more youth soccer parks, forcing those sports to work harder to create their next generation of players. But while as many as sixty million American children play the game, the United States remains the great untapped market for soccer.

If you read the papers or watched the news prior to the 2006 World Cup, you could well be excused for thinking soccer in America was a recent phenomenon, perhaps stretching as far back as 1999 and that Women's World Cup. You might even have asked—as one brave reporter at a news conference with the men's team did—why Mia Hamm wasn't out on the field this year.*

In fact soccer has been a part of the American landscape since the turn of the twentieth century, but it has always struggled to gain a foothold as a spectator sport. Like many other turn-of-the-century sporting vogues, such as boxing and horse racing, soccer was once enjoyed by many working people. But, unlike those entertainments, soccer was rarely presented as a fully professional sport, and therein lies a story about as American as it gets.

Soccer was carried into the United States by a number of immigrant groups. The most dominant groups, the British and Irish, who played the game up and down the eastern seaboard, quickly seized control of the sport at the grassroots level and to this day imagine themselves as defenders and arbiters of the American game. But this "British mafia," as one Canadian soccer administrator colorfully put it, was hardly the only group with a stake in the sport. Greek and Portuguese immigrants took to the game rapidly as well, and soccer enclaves sprang up in West Indian, Scandinavian, Italian, and Latin American communities. For years, these groups tugged at one another at the state level, playing matches in patchwork leagues at parks and rec facilities across the United States. Sadly for the game's acceptance, these ethnic groups were shockingly insular; instead of their shared love of a sport acting as a glue between the groups, it served instead to push

---

*Here's how out of touch the mainstream media is with the sport: At a conference previewing a World Cup qualification match against Trinidad and Tobago, one reporter asked why the USA had "to play two games in one day." She went on to opine that this seemed unfair.

them farther apart. Such ethnic friction also served to keep the game out of the mainstream.*

In this information age, people forget just how cut off the United States was from the rest of the soccer world. Information on world soccer leagues was almost nonexistent in the mainstream papers before the late 1990s, and gaining access to reports on leagues we consider "major" today—such as Italy and Germany—required learning languages, buying a shortwave radio, and collecting elusive copies of foreign newspapers. In the mid-1970s I learned a few words of Portuguese so I could purchase *A Bola* for my father; my dinners

_____

*Consider the state of the game as it was in Hartford, Connecticut, in the 1970s. Connecticut—along with New York and New Jersey—has contributed an inordinate number of soccer administrators to the top levels of the American game. Sunil Gulati, the current president of U.S. Soccer, the governing body for the American sport, grew up in Connecticut as an immigrant from India, and both played and refereed the game before becoming involved in its management. He took a career path that many people followed (including, it should be noted, members of my own family), from a love of the game at the grassroots level to the sport's management. In those days, that usually entailed organizing and running one of the many state ethnic teams. There were the Hartford Hellenic, the Italian-American Stars, one to three teams for the Portuguese (depending on the state of the political unrest), and clubs for the English, Irish, Peruvians, Argentines, and Poles. Soccer in the state was colorful and occasionally maddening.

The state organization was overseen by U.S. Soccer hall of famer Bertil Larsen, a chauvinistic Swedish American for whom the word *colorful* is insufficient. One of the tamer stories involving Larsen recounts his showing up at a rec park site only to discover that city workers had planted a telephone pole in the middle of the pitch. He promptly called both local papers to rage that "this sort of [expletive] thing would never have happened in Sweden." Perhaps not, but the story illustrates just how out-of-touch these weekend leagues were. Nonetheless, these leagues were the backbone of what would come to be the national team program in the United States (and the proving ground for a World Cup referee, Dave Socha, a Massachusetts native who worked two of the top events).

were spent listening to obscure league matches from exotic countries on shortwave. My father and his brother would team up to make regular trips to New York's major newsstands and come home laden with copies of *La Gazzetta dello Sport, Guerin Sportivo, L'Equipe,* and the *Times* of London. For a time, my father was one of two people in the United States who had a subscription to *France Football.* I was the other.

We cut lineups from games out of these papers and pasted them into ratty three-ring binders with rubber cement, the smell of which can still make me think of the English first division.* For a long time, these homemade tomes were our Torah, the only records we would ever have on players from faraway lands. There is a peculiar reward in learning enough of a language to be able to understand a game's call, and a pure, if stupid, joy in recognizing the announcers and becoming distant acquaintances with the men who brought Mexican, Russian, and Spanish soccer into our house. When soccer finally came to the big screens of closed-circuit television, there was the thrill of putting faces to those voices.

Today, soccer is so much more widely available, and so much of it is broadcast in the game's new lingua franca, English, that it must seem baffling that people would go to such great lengths just to figure out what was going on in the Belgian second division. There was another aspect to the pursuit, however, that was often more rewarding than the game

---

*The Premier League did not exist until the 1990s; the old first division was the top tier of the sport in England. I mention this because, should you look at the scores from today's "first division," you're likely to be confused. Today's first division is actually the *third* division of the sport in that country.

itself. Back then, to find out about the world's game you had to walk through neighborhoods and make friends. You had to ask the Portuguese coffee shop that got copies of *A Bola* to hold one for you each week. You had to find an Italian deli that would make sure you got copies of *Tuttosport*. Maybe you'd trade reel-to-reel tapes of games back and forth across the Atlantic, and when the VCR revolution came into being you had to find friends in Europe who would tape and trade games with you. Ironically, considering the insularity of many ethnic leagues in the United States at the time, for fans passionate about the European or South American game, soccer meant reaching out to the world and breaking down ethnic barriers.

Not so for another group of American soccer fans at this time, who were overwhelmingly white, suburban, and middle class. Their soccer interests were definitely focused on this side of the Atlantic and the Northern Hemisphere. The game they supported was soccer, but only after a fashion.

Soccer has been a staple of East Coast schools since the 1930s, but this version of the game has vastly different rules. While the international game is a test of endurance and skill, the American school game evolved into a helter-skelter exhibition of speed and effort, because coaches are allowed to make nearly unfettered substitutions. One of the early adherents of this bastardization of the game was University of Connecticut coach Joe Morrone, who saw it as an "American version" of the world's game. He was but one of many who, over the years, have embraced ideas like eliminating ties in order to make the game more palatable for American audiences. The NASL would do the same, with thirty-five-yard lines, Astroturf, and commercial breaks. Even MLS began with a ludicrous combination of on-field clocks and giant flags for a tiebreaker "shoot-out."*

The next group of American soccer fans is also, from my point of view, one of the most peculiar. These are the youth fans, exemplified by the American Youth Soccer Organization (AYSO). In the 1970s parents across the United States pulled their kids out of Pop Warner football and Little League and stuck them into soccer on the notion that the game was "less violent." Anyone who's seen a game knows this is a bizarre idea, but the crux here is that all of a sudden soccer in the United States went from being a "sport" to an "activity."

The two are very different. A sport is a contest. Some people are better than others, somebody wins, somebody loses. In the gauzy view of the 1970s, soccer was retrofitted to make it a game where everyone got a chance to play and everyone got a trophy for showing up. Everyone was special— and therefore no one was special. Soccer became a symbol of liberal excess, and while it's a stretch to call this activity "Communist" (as some did at the time), it's pretty clear that a game in which everyone gets to play and everyone wins is not really a sport.

This version of soccer lives on today in the well-meaning AYSO. AYSO has, according to its third-quarter 2005 financial statements, some 582,225 members and a budget of just over

---

*Americans—like anyone else—enjoy putting their stamp on sports. American football, is, after all, a derivation of soccer. Brazil has a game called *futsal,* which is something akin to indoor soccer, though it is played on a hardwood floor. *Futevolei* is a soccer/volleyball cross popular in Brazil, Holland, and France. Need we bring up baseball and its relationship to rounders?

$14 million annually, and took in about $6.8 million in fees in 2005. It also has some $1.7 million in the bank in assets and a good handful of sponsors that includes MLS and the U.S. Soccer Foundation. While not gargantuan by today's standards, AYSO is a healthy nonprofit. Youth soccer, as espoused by AYSO, is the antithesis of the high-pressure player development that can still be found in some kids' football, basketball, and baseball leagues. In fact, the organization forms new teams each year, because, as its Web site puts it: "It is fair and more fun when teams of equal ability play."

That brings us to the second version of youth soccer that exists in the United States. Like the AYSO, competitive youth soccer is largely a suburban phenomenon, one where "travel" and "select" teams on the Olympic Development Program (ODP) track charge parents a great deal of money to develop their children, especially girls, into possible collegiate stars. This effort is worthwhile because one of the biggest effects of Title IX has been a dramatic increase in funding for women's soccer programs, allowing young women to take advantage of the athletic largesse once the sole purview of boys. Smart parents have since realized that it makes good sense for young women to chase a soccer scholarship and a great many smart young women are able to get free rides at top schools simply for being decent soccer players. Specializing in soccer isn't such a great plan if you're a young man.

Highly competitive programs such as the select teams— a number of which are organized under the banner of U.S. Youth Soccer, a nonprofit formed in 1974 that also offers programs catering to the "just-for-fun" kids—have contributed to the current crop of MLS and national team players. But there are certain real difficulties with the setup as far as player development goes. College soccer is still a different game, and the ODP programs are clearly restricted to a higher economic level.

Overseas, players are recruited by clubs and then brought up through the club's system at no cost to the players' families. As Europeans and Latin Americans have de-emphasized school sports, such club soccer is usually the only vehicle available for high-quality games. In America, the cost of player development being largely borne by parents has had the unfortunate side effect of leaving out kids who are too poor to play, economically and racially segregating the sport. Youth soccer in the United States is overwhelmingly white,* and the disconnect between African American players and their white counterparts is shocking at times. On the 2006 American World Cup team, the black players—DaMarcus Beasley, Eddie Pope, and Eddie Johnson—kept to themselves, joined only by Clint Dempsey, who grew up in an overwhelmingly black neighborhood. When I asked Dempsey about this, he said the guys felt they didn't have much in common with the other players.

Noting these downsides of youth soccer brings a lot of heat.† Youth soccer families often bring a missionary's zeal to the sport. More than one parent has told me with a straight face that if more kids just played soccer, the world would be a better place. And woe to the person who questions the ability of these young players—this "game" is all about affirmation;

---

*Steven Wells wrote an interesting and much-discussed column on this in the June 17, 2005, edition of the *Manchester Guardian.*
†I know. I foolishly wrote about this topic in my second column for Fox and received over one thousand e-mails.

challenging that is tantamount to apostasy. Fans of the youth and "American" game refer to critics as "Eurosnobs."

This fragmentation of the sport's fan base in the United States—into the ethnic base, the suburban faction, and the overwhelmingly privileged competitive players—has had clear beneficiaries: other sports.

No wonder, then, that today's standard bearers for the professional game in America have looked to corporate America to help pay the bills. However, while an organization such as MLS hopes to gain national and international legitimacy by tying Budweiser and Chevrolet to its product, most major advertisers correctly see the American sport as a niche market. While NFL owners are snapping up English soccer clubs at bargain prices, MLS has trouble selling ten thousand tickets a game.* The women's national team, heroes for a brief moment in 1999, are back to playing in almost empty stadiums.† And soccer fans themselves, confronted with an overwhelming number of cable channels dedicated to the international sport, have fractured the pro sport's base. After all, why pay $100 to take the family to see an MLS game when you can see every game from the English Premier League for $11.99 a month?

----

*This is according to internal ticket sales documents. While MLS touts average attendances in excess of sixteen thousand, over a third of those seats are apparently given away.
†Infamously, the women's professional league—which managed to burn through some $60 million in seed money in one astonishing season—announced it was going out of business with a conference call that begged for corporate support!

Used to playing obscure matches in half-full American arenas, a number of Team USA players found the difference in Gelsenkirchen jarring.

Even on TV, on a giant screen in a park, you could tell the arena was deafening. The crowd was overwhelmingly Czech,* and with the Czech supporters filling the air with shouts of *"Czechi Czechi!"* at kickoff, the USA was immediately rattled. Oguchi Onyewu took a yellow card just four minutes in when he cut the legs out from under Pavel Nedvěd. But it was on the ensuing play that things broke down for good. Keller saved the free-kick well, but released the ball downfield too quickly for his forwards. The Czech center-backs saw Zdeněk Grygera streaking down the flank, and with a long pass, sprung him. Grygera raced past Mastroeni, and served the ball into the mountainous Jan Koller, who easily beat Eddie Pope and Keller with a fine header. Just like that, the game was over. As Koller raced away toward the sideline, eyes bulging and arms raised in triumph, Keller lay on the turf, on his side. His eyes betrayed his professional calm: The sparkle was gone.

The rest of the game was a showcase for Tomáš Rosický, a gifted Czech midfielder who glided around the park and iced the match with a thirty-yard screamer before the half ended. He would put another one off the crossbar late in the match before scoring the finale with just fifteen minutes left to go. After the goal, Rosický soared toward the center of the field, his face lit with childlike glee. Rosický had just become a star, and in his wake he left a shambles in blue shirts, and a

*Best moment: the canny fan, dressed in Czech red, who had brought his blow-up doll with him dressed up in a full Czech kit. He parked it on the seat next to him.

goalkeeper sitting disconsolately on the turf, wondering what had happened.

Ironically, in 1990 the USA had debuted in the modern era at the World Cup and lost to the then Czechoslovakia 5–1. But then, no one noticed. On June 12, 2006, the whole world saw it. Despite the hype, this American team just plain failed to deliver on the night.

A furious Arena publicly lambasted his team postgame, singling out Landon Donovan and DaMarcus Beasley in an unusually wide-ranging and personal critique of the side's shortcomings.

On Bobby Convey: "He at least had the courage to attack, one of the few players who did."

On Landon Donovan: "He showed no aggressiveness."

On DaMarcus Beasley: "We got nothing from him."

The players went ballistic. Beasley was the first to fire back at his coach, saying that Arena's unexpectedly switching him into a defensive role meant he couldn't attack.

"I don't know what he wants me to do," Beasley said bitterly.

Arena's response? "If he [Beasley] is any kind of a player or a man," said Arena, "he understands that [criticism]. If he doesn't, he's not going to be in a position to help us in games two or three either."

Convey noted that, from his perspective, Arena was quick to take credit when things went right, but quick to blame the team when it lost. Convey also stunned reporters by saying the team "didn't know what to do" in its first game despite years of intensive preparation: "I think the reason why we didn't do well is because everyone did not do their role, maybe didn't know their role, maybe didn't know what to do."

Arena denied that, saying: "Our guys know everything going into these games. They are thoroughly prepared for these games, but it could be a case where we were over-organized."

Fans stateside woke up to all these harsh words in their newspapers and on TV. The 2006 World Cup was enjoying a huge increase in TV viewership and attention in the States, and a feeling of betrayal was evident even half the world away. The American team had finally gotten what it wanted—mainstream attention—and discovered there *is* such a thing as bad publicity. With the USA seemingly in free fall, Arena said glumly, "If I had to do it over again, I'm not sure there's a whole lot I would change."

Watching all this from the bench was Clint Dempsey in his first World Cup. "It was terrible. I just wanted to get in and help, to do something."

A darkly handsome man, Dempsey looks somewhat sour and menacing on the field. His eyes are heavy-lidded but bright, and his gaze is always fixed a few feet beyond where you think it should be. Off the field, he's soft-spoken and friendly. In games, he's ruthless.

Dempsey grew up in Nacogdoches, Texas, where he and his older brother Ryan learned the game from a neighboring Mexican family. Unlike a lot of kids playing soccer in the United States, the Dempsey boys weren't suburban and weren't rich.

I once asked Ryan to describe a little of Nacogdoches for me.

"Well, there's not much to describe," said Ryan. "We were in a trailer park. I guess you could say it was the wrong side of the tracks. I dunno, there really isn't much to Nacogdoches at all."

Clint's first real team was a youth side called the Dallas Texans. Ryan was trying out for the team, and Clint was killing time juggling a soccer ball while waiting. The coach saw him, and he got invited to play as well. Once he got the bug, Clint's whole life came to revolve around the sport.

As soon as he was old enough, he would travel four hours round-trip to Dallas to play. That was where the best team was, and the Dempsey boys always wanted to play against the best. "I had to get a tape deck for those rides," says Clint, "they were so long. The good thing is that's how I fell in love with music, but it was a long ride."

The Dempseys had to work hard just to play their sport, and there were other difficulties, too. Their sister, Jennifer, died suddenly of a brain aneurysm at the age of sixteen. Money was tight—getting Clint and Ryan out to games required the family to sell their boat and take on extra jobs. And life in the trailer park was hard and dull; the boys had few friends and spent a lot of their time trying to pull in games on TV.

"One of us would be up on the roof of the trailer with this crappy dish," said Ryan, "and we'd be yelling back and forth, moving the dish, trying to find something. And one of us would see this thing on TV, and we knew it was a game— it looked like a game, through all the snow and shit, and we'd sit there right up against the TV, trying to make it out. It was ridiculous. We did this, like, every day."

Unusual for Americans, perhaps, the Dempseys also grew up color-blind. One of Clint's closest friends was the rapper Big Hawk. When Clint was given the opportunity to record a song as part of Nike's ad campaign for the 2006 World Cup, he did it because Big Hawk and his other friends could make a buck or two off the recording and producing. They didn't have long to enjoy it: After the track came out, Hawk was shot and killed in downtown Houston. The crime remains unsolved, and Hawk's death hit the Dempseys hard.

But Clint is a religious man. In fact, he says if he hadn't become a soccer player, he would have become a priest. A lot of athletes talk about God, but Clint, who radiates a rather soothing sense of faith, is one of the few who doesn't sound like he's blowing smoke when he does it.

"My whole life, I had to work for everything," says Clint. "I've been blessed that it has worked out for me; I have been lucky for the things that have gone my way, and for the things that didn't, well, I was humbled by them. Having a sister pass away lit a fire under me, and I have never given up.

"You can get so caught up in soccer sometimes, worrying over a bad game or a bad performance. A couple of years ago, I was nowhere, and I broke my jaw in a game and I thought I might be done—I had been invited to the national team, and I was just praying to the Lord to get another opportunity after that. I really had to take a step back and remind myself of all the things that have happened, and realize that what I'm doing, playing soccer, is just a game. There's something after this life that's more important than that.

"So, when I got chosen for the World Cup squad, I had a whole different perspective—I didn't feel any pressure. I had already dealt with pressure."

He was perhaps the only one. And his moment was about to come.

INTERLUDE:
WHEN SOCCER WAS IMPORTANT

There was a time when soccer was a big game in the States. It was a brief moment that came out of nowhere, only to vanish almost overnight. Most people don't remember the North American Soccer League as a vibrant, twenty-four-team enterprise that played coast to coast. Nor do they remember the regional success teams such as the Tampa Bay Rowdies, the Washington Diplomats, and the Chicago Sting had. But they do remember Pelé, and they remember the New York Cosmos, which was the first—and perhaps last—hint of what American soccer could someday be.

The New York Cosmos never made a dime. The league they raised from nothing to popularity is now dust. But the legacy the team left is one of true greatness. The Cosmos are one of the best-known sides in the history of the sport, recognized worldwide as the team of Pelé, Carlos Alberto, Giorgio Chinaglia, and Franz Beckenbauer. And despite the perception of the United States as woefully bereft when it comes to the game the world calls football, the Cosmos were a uniquely American invention that inarguably laid the groundwork for today's super clubs such as Manchester United and Real Madrid.

Soccer's American moment came in 1977. It was a year of tremendous hardship in New York. Reeling from budget shortfalls and urban poverty, New York was seen far and wide as a magnet for depravity and crime. Heroin use was eating the inner city alive, and the murder total for the year approached two thousand. The Big Apple was on edge from the as-yet-unsolved Son of Sam slayings, in which six people were killed and seven wounded. And when a heat wave knocked power out for twenty-five hours in July, sending New Yorkers into the sweltering streets, looting and violence engulfed Brooklyn, Harlem, and the South Bronx. July 13 would be dubbed "the Night of Terror" by *Time* magazine.

New York was a city that needed a distraction, and it ended up finding solace in a most unusual team.

Despite the fact that 1977 saw the New York Yankees win the World Series again—this time behind the bat of Reggie Jackson and his famous three home-run performance in Game Six against the Los Angeles Dodgers—the Yankees weren't the hottest ticket in town. Nor were the Mets, Knicks, or Rangers.

Believe it or not (and many couldn't) that ticket was to see the New York Cosmos, who just two years earlier had been a ragtag group playing at a decrepit Randall's Island stadium in a league effectively run by five people from a dingy Park Avenue office.

Four men had been responsible for changing how the American sport was perceived. Clive Toye, an English expat and former writer for the *Daily Express,* dreamed of signing the greatest player the world had ever known and making the game come alive in the United States. Steve Ross of Warner Communications and Ahmet Ertegün of Atlantic Records put up the money to turn a joke into a phenomenon. The final, and most important, man was Edson Arantes do Nascimento, better known as Pelé.

The NASL came into a fitful existence in 1967, out of the ashes of the United Soccer Association and an outlaw league called the National Premier Soccer League (NPSL). Barely registering on the sports radar at the time, the NPSL had been unable to parlay the exposure it received on the CBS television network into attendance in the stands. Toye—who had been in the States on and off since 1961, covering the Canada Cup golf tourney and boxing matches—had accepted an offer to become the general manager of the Baltimore Bays following the 1966 World Cup. When the NPSL collapsed the next year, Toye and Phil Woosnam, once a Welsh International and then the general manager and player coach of the Atlanta Chiefs, created the NASL. In 1969, with NFL owner Lamar Hunt bankrolling the league, Woosnam became commissioner. The NASL operated at a subsistence level with five teams and the small Park Avenue office. It was hardly a glamorous life.

"When we started up again, Phil and I sat down and talked about the things we wanted to do, which included staging the World Cup in the United States, signing Pelé, getting a team in New York, running a youth development program—in retrospect, all ideas that if anyone had heard, they would have thought we were mad," says Toye.

But the ideas didn't die, and in 1971 the Cosmos were birthed when Woosnam met the Ertegün brothers, Nesuhi and Ahmet, at a cocktail party in Mexico City. Jay Emmett, who was legal counsel for Warner Communications, recalls that the Ertegüns, along with eight other men, put up $35,000 apiece for the expansion fee.

"I got interested because I thought there would be licensing and market deals to be had," says Emmett. "We got into soccer because Nesuhi and Ahmet were important to Warner. We said to ourselves that you've got three million kids playing soccer, that mothers love it, and that it wasn't an expensive sport. We thought it would translate to America well. Of course, it never happened."

Toye chose the team name as a play on the name of the recently born expansion baseball team, the New York Metropolitans. "I said, 'What's bigger than Metropolitans? Cosmopolitans!' But I couldn't call them that, so I chose Cosmos," says Toye. "The owners objected, but they weren't paying real close attention in those difficult early years and so the name stuck."

English coach Gordon Bradley ran the side and the club bounced from Yankee Stadium to a complex at Hofstra University, to the aging Downing Stadium on Randall's Island.

"It was hideous," says former Cosmos star Werner Roth of Downing. "There was no glamour at Randall's—the dressing room leaked from the ceiling, and it was pretty dank."

Meanwhile, Toye nursed his dream of signing Pelé, who was winding down a fabled career with Santos of Brazil. Toye struck up a friendship with the superstar in 1973 following a match between Chelsea and Santos staged in Kingston, Jamaica. "I told him that he had to come to America, because he would have the chance to do something no one else could do, which was make soccer a major sport in the USA. Pelé later admitted he had no idea what the hell I was talking about."

Getting Pelé was not a smooth process.

"Getting him to play again," said Toye, "that was the biggest difficulty. He offered to let us use his name, play exhibitions, and all that and I had to explain over and over again that that wasn't good enough. He was the only one who could break through the crust of indifference. At that time, even the un-washed American public had some idea that this guy in Brazil was the best player in the world, so I kept on. I was close to giv-ing up after years of this when I think he realized life was dif-ferent without playing soccer—the money does not come in. Then Juventus and Real Madrid were nibbling at him in Febru-ary of that year, and I said if you go there, all you can do is win a championship; if you come here, you can win a country. He and he alone could do something no one had ever done and bring the sport into the mainstream. That worked. He signed."

The signing took place in Bermuda ("for tax reasons," says Emmett) and went in fits and starts.

Pelé would finally make his appearance in America in the summer of 1975. Toye recalls that "all of a sudden, we had more media attention on one day than we had had in the pre-vious five years.

"We went from this tiny club run by five people to suddenly now one of the biggest in the world. In terms of media atten-tion, we're huge, getting three or four thousand people calling. We were inundated. None of us slept for the next five days. The best part was that we had to go up to Randall's with green spray paint because we were going to be on CBS that afternoon and we needed the field to look green. We painted the mud."

Roth recalls Pelé's arrival: "He landed in a helicopter at the horseshoe end of Randall's Island. All these people were around watching him, and he watched the game from the stands. It was terrible."

The press box was high school size, the parking lot nearly nonexistent, and so many fans came that they double-parked on the one bridge linking the island with Manhattan. The police didn't seem to notice.

"I think Robert Redford came the first year," says Toye. "But big shots were not coming to Randall's, not with the men's toilets leaking down to the floor below."

And then the Cosmos—with Pelé in tow—got the go-ahead to play at Giants Stadium.

"It happened rather quickly," says Roth. "We get Pelé, we move to Giants, and on opening day we draw forty to forty-five thousand and then have our first sellout right after that. It was a little intimidating. Then it became empowering."*

The Cosmos happened to arrive on the scene at the right time, for the city was undergoing a sea change. New York had always been the immigrant capital of the United States; now its ethnic enclaves began to flex not only political but social muscle. For a young boy riding around the city, New York was a colorful Babylon, from the wild-style graffiti subway cars to the *nueva latina* beat pulsing through East Harlem. At night, whole city blocks would go dark as promoters presided over giant parties with DJs such as Joseph Saddler—better known as Grandmaster Flash—wiring their decks right into the city street lamps. Boom boxes blasting bootleg mix tapes by the likes of Kool DJ Herc and DJ Hollywood filled the city streets and parks.

Disco was king in the "respectable" clubs, with Studio 54

---

*For the record, the well-meaning Roth is factually incorrect here: The Cosmos averaged 18,227 fans in 1976 and there were no sellouts until the 1977 playoffs.

being ground zero and one of the home bases for the players. Says Roth, "It was pretty standard Cosmos treatment. The mob would part, the velvet ropes come open, and you'd be taken into a banquette or VIP room there, which at Studio 54 were open to us at any time. We got superstar treatment."

New York Post writer Phil Mushnick, who began his career covering the Cosmos, recalls how players were able to take advantage of that. "Francisco Marinho got suspended for getting nabbed with two women in bed with him at the Hasbrook Heights Hilton. They called him 'Mezzaninho' because he would always hit the ball thirty-five yards over the bar into the decks. And Pelé was always on lobby duty, looking to get laid. We called him a 'secret agent.' It was all Hollywood."

The Cosmos became a team drenched in celebrity.

"There'd be Carly Simon and Mick Jagger, Peter Frampton—just walking past you," says Ray Hudson, one of the great English imports into the league. "It was astounding. I was a choirboy—these were bigger personalities and names than I'd seen in Newcastle."

Hudson recalls showing up at Giants Stadium with his team, the Fort Lauderdale Strikers, to survey the scene. "I was twenty-two, and I'm like shit—I'm playing against Pelé. I mean, I would go to the park with my crucifix hanging out pretending to be him. It was such an honor. After the match, Pelé had promised me his shirt, and I went into the locker room and there was Ahmet on his knees giving Pelé's feet a rub. I wish I'd had a camera."

"That locker room had everyone. Mario Cuomo, Kissinger, the Monty Python guys. It was a tough room to work in, actually," says Mushnick. "I had to blow off Mick Jagger four times! Mick used to come up to me and say the same thing every game—mbleh mblah blah blah—and I could never understand a goddamn word."

"Ahmet brought everyone who was anyone into that locker room," recalls Roth. "And every arrogant loud rock and roller turned to a pontificating little boy in front of Pelé—except for Alice Cooper; he wound up wearing Pelé's shirt on stage. It was funny—these obviously successful, wealthy people that were like little boys in front of him."

The addition in 1977 of the great former West German captain Franz Beckenbauer solidified the team's international reputation.

"Beckenbauer was incredible," says Mushnick. "We were on a trip, I think we came to Rochester, New York, which he referred to as a 'potato field,' and Hank Gola and I and Eric Mortensen were playing one of those new tabletop video games. Beckenbauer walked in and watched two games, and asked if he could try it. He was on that game with a first quarter for an hour. The average time for us was something like six minutes."

Giants Stadium saw a strong string of games—seventy thousand people were showing up to see a team that two years before had had trouble drawing five thousand. In just one year, attendance jumped by almost fifty thousand people—in 1976 the biggest crowd the Cosmos had was 27,892; August 14, 1977 saw 77,691 show up for a playoff game against the Strikers.

The NASL reaped the benefits that year: The Tampa Bay Rowdies drew 62,394 one day in June and the Los Angeles Aztecs pulled in 57,191 at the Rose Bowl around the same time.

The Cosmos weren't just the toast of the town—they were the toast of the sport.

And there's where the problems began.

"Ross became obsessed," says Toye ruefully. "And because he was, all of a sudden Warner executives came out of the woodwork. We had all kinds of people making all kinds of ridiculous fucking decisions and suggestions and making the thing a laughingstock internally. We had one stupid little asshole trying to tell us that we have to change the way the game starts. He wanted it to be like the Harlem Globetrotters— have Pelé juggling the ball for five minutes, Beckenbauer for five minutes in the center circle—like a circus act. I told him that wouldn't work because not only would these great players not do that, but the other nine guys on the field couldn't juggle the ball."

The volatile Ross was so taken with his creation he had a seat belt installed at his chair at Giants Stadium to keep himself off the field. He needed it. "We had to play a game under protest one time because he thought the ref had disallowed two goals unfairly," says Toye. "He wanted to go into the dressing room and tell the guys not to come out for the second half. I had to go on the PA and announce we were playing the second half under protest. It was humiliating. Of course, we end up winning 5–3."

There were also outbreaks of . . . weirdness. "[Midfielder Johan] Neeskens spent a flight to a game on the charter in drag," says Mushnick. "He had the lipstick, the dress on, and then he stuck golf balls in his shirt. It was originally funny, but then it became uncomfortable. He stayed in drag the whole damn flight."

Goalkeeper Shep Messing had already been kicked off the team for a period in 1974 after accepting $5,000 to pose for

Viva magazine,* exposure the Cosmos decided they could do without.

South African coach Eddie Firmani arrived midway through 1977 to replace the popular Bradley, who had steered the team since 1971, when he signed on as player coach. (Bradley had been relieved for a brief interval in 1976 by fellow Englishman Ken Furphy, but had later returned.)

"Firmani had such an odd idea about the media," says Mushnick. "Just after he was signed, he approached me and Hank Gola in a hotel and said, 'I have this watch. Could you take it downtown to get it repaired?'"

But a greater harbinger of change would be the emergence of recent addition Giorgio Chinaglia as a general off the field.

"I didn't come just to play soccer," says Chinaglia, who joined from Rome club Lazio and would become the most prolific scorer in the history of the NASL. "I was twenty-seven and my wife at the time was an American. Steve Ross and I were friends, but I was a player and an executive, too, so it was a double burden. What I tried to do was get the best American players. I knew that we had to do that and get the best young Americans competing against the best in the world, just as is happening now. In my day it was unthinkable for Americans to play against Pelé or to go overseas."

Chinaglia, who today works in broadcasting, had an arrest warrant issued for him by the Italian authorities on October 13, 2006, in connection with charges of insider trading

---

*Messing sometimes claims in interviews that he posed in the better-known *Playgirl* and was paid $10,000. (See John Genzale's article in the *Chicago Sun-Times* of July 14, 2006.) *Viva* is also sometimes incorrectly referred to as a sister publication of *Playgirl;* it was actually a competing publication put out by Bob Guccione of *Penthouse*.

and extortion relating to an attempt to purchase his old club team, Lazio. He denied these charges when I contacted him about them. Chinaglia remains a controversial figure today, just as he was on the field.

"Of all the players getting introduced at a game," says Hudson, "you'd hear the name *Chinaglia*, and these boos would rain down. It was a real nerve jangler. It was funny— we all thought the world of him. It was like *Gladiator*, the cascade of boos and then of course he'd score, and go to the crowd beating on his chest and the crowd would go nuts."

"Chinaglia was an enormous pain in the ass," says Toye. "I wrote a memo to Emmett once—one of the few humans left in the office then—about him saying that I'd done what I had done well and had been left alone, and if they didn't want me to do that anymore, then I'd leave. Well, two-thirds of the way through [1977], I left, and they carried on. And then soon after, Gordon Bradley left. And then it was history."

"There were some clashes of culture," says Mushnick. "We were in Seattle in July after Firmani took over and we were going to practice in the Kingdome and one guy hadn't shown up yet. It was Pelé, he was late. Once Pelé got on the bus, Eddie stood up and said in his clipped South African accent, 'Now this is what we don't want.'"

Pelé would retire after the 1977 season, and the NASL began to get saddled with a reputation for over-the-hill talent. Compounding the league's problems was the taste for expansion it acquired following its success in New York. "The league had a rush of blood to the head and went insane," says Mushnick. And there was that little fact that the Cosmos never made money.

"We had hoped Pelé would drive some stuff. We met with Pepsi, I think," says Emmett. "Nothing happened."

"We held costs down," says Toye, "but after a while, there were so many owners, and players would just go talk to their 'owner,' and when players have access to the top echelon, you have disaster. I think a lot of harm was done by the gross excesses of the Cosmos after my days, because I kept a tight handle on the budget."

The league never recovered, and Toye, in fact, was called back in to try and rescue it in 1984. But he couldn't.

"I played against New York at Minneapolis, as the Strikers had moved to play indoors," recalls Hudson. "It was to be an indoor/outdoor league. I remember Giorgio saying that the party was over. It was like playing in front of a church procession. These people are banging into the boards and against the Perspex [acrylic glass], but the fans were like, 'What's this?' When they started playing indoors, that was the death knell."

Entertainment was also changing in America.

Soccer would limp on, indoors and out, until 1994, with the American World Cup. Today, the team in New York is called Red Bull New York, after its owner, the Austrian soft drink maker. MLS is in its twelfth year and is still enduring America's ability to ignore it.

Thirty years later, the team most people recall when they think of soccer in New York is the Cosmos.

"We were known worldwide," says Chinaglia, and he is not lying. The Cosmos was the team of not just a city, but an entire sport.

6

ILL HEALTH, HEROES, AND HEARTBREAK

When I was a kid, my mother forced me to bundle up in ludicrously oversized clothing to guard against chills. I looked like an overripe, wobbly blackberry in my blue snowsuit, which was absolutely the worst-designed garment ever made for a child. Its closely woven nylon hermetically sealed and turned the sweat-soaked wearer into a plump little cocktail wiener. I wanted to get out of the damn thing as fast as possible. This 1970s-era contraption of straps, buttons, and snaps was also almost impossible to put on—Mom usually got the thing halfway on me, said the hell with it, and sent me tottering off to school. Did I mention the hood was so tight I could only see straight ahead?

I thought of this snowsuit in the dead heat of June because I was forced to make several visits to German pharmacies, all of which seemed to specialize in "drafts and chills" protections and remedies, usually in the form of foul-tasting teas. Never before had I suspected the horror stray gusts of air could cause a population, but judging from the stockpiles of natural and/or homeopathic remedies that lined row after row of dark-stained wood shelves, chills are a serious, perhaps deadly, problem particular to Bavaria. There were other weird ailments I had never heard of: A German friend told me people suffered from *horsturz,* which is apparently stress-induced hearing loss, and something truly awful-sounding, *kreislaufzusammenbruch*—or "circulatory collapse"!* If my circulation collapsed, I think I'd be dead. Apparently in Germany this means you take the day off. These folks are either extremely hardy or very foolhardy, and I'm not sure which.

Unfortunately, my needs were not so easily met. I suffer from epilepsy,[†] and German customs officials had seized my medications—I take a cocktail of four distinct anti-convulsants—on the grounds that it is illegal to import pharmaceuticals that could be obtained in Germany.[‡] A full week of pleading with the German authorities, and having

---

*I thought this was a joke. Apparently, it's not: After doing a bit of digging, I found a great many references to these conditions and their treatments. *Der Spiegel* even wrote a very funny little article on this for World Cup visitors, partly to reassure them if and when their hosts mentioned these awful-sounding ailments.

[†]Today, this would properly be called a "seizure disorder," but having had this for over thirty-five years, I'm sticking with the old-school term.

[‡]There also was a bit of "cultural difference" at work here. Many Germans apparently do not believe in medication per se and seek "natural" alternatives, and Americans are viewed as grotesquely overmedicated pill poppers. The customs agents, perhaps not entirely believing that someone would *really* take thirty-five pills a day, probably seized them on these quasi-moral grounds combined with their faint suspicion that I might attempt to distribute these pills to fallen members of their population. This was ridiculous. A junkie I know once told me: "Dude, I'd never put that stuff in my body." When a guy who is comfortable shooting up shit acquired on the street from a guy named Boo Boo pales at your meds, you know they're undesirable.

some World Cup officials plead on my behalf, came to naught. And so, in the second week of the tournament, I fell dangerously ill.*

After hysterical transatlantic phone calls, faxed prescriptions, consultations with German doctors, and the unleashing of the unholy furor that one's spouse can deliver in times of crisis, a cowed local pharmacist agreed that, yes, it would be better if I were not in convulsions on his floor, and actually filled a prescription with something other than leaves in a bag.

Other familiar processes were also a little different in Germany.

To get a press credential to cover the World Cup, you go through a three-step process that ensures FIFA maximum control over game access. First, you go through a background check, and a quite exhaustive one at that. Washington has had a file on me open since 1996, when I covered the Atlanta Olympic Games, and over the years I have received a handful of calls from nice but firm gentlemen who have asked precise, unvarnished questions about my global travel. In the spring of 2006, a next-door neighbor whom I did not know well disappeared from our neighborhood. Three or four days later, I came out to get the paper at an unusually early hour and found a number of automatic weapons pointed at me and at his house. The neighbor turned out to have been smuggling guns, and, in the course of investigating him, the FBI took statements from all of us who lived nearby. I subsequently got several follow-up calls from a polite gentleman who seemed

---

*See the end of this book and the acknowledgments for the aftereffects of this. Just for the record, I'm much better now, thanks.

skeptical that I would go to El Salvador and Guatemala purely for "sohcker,"* as he put it.

One week into the tournament, my cell phone rang as I was headed to the market. It was my "friend" from the FBI, who was "just following up" on my neighbor's case—it seemed he had fled into Mexico, but might I have seen him? When I explained that I was standing in downtown Munich, this threw the agent for a second, until he remembered this "whole World Cup thing" was going on. We chatted for a few minutes, and he mentioned he had seen the USA's loss to the Czechs written up in the local paper. Then there was a pause, and he said, "So, that Pelé's quite a guy, huh?"

The second stage of getting a credential is being vetted by the local federation. If you are like me and have written a number of pieces that question the federation's ability to do its job in a reliable manner, you are denied. The third stage of getting a credential is then to appeal directly to FIFA in Zurich, making note of just how many of its tournaments you have covered. There is actually a formula that takes into account youth and women's tournaments as well as senior men's events, and the more of these you cover, the better level of access you are granted. Thus, if you looked carefully at my badge at the 2006 World Cup, you would have noticed that I was officially Swiss and therefore at the top of the pecking order. And so, while my American colleagues had a rough time getting tickets to matches, in many cases I glided right in. Yes, it's small and petty, but I took some pleasure in this.

---

*After spending time in Mazatenango, where tires are burned in the middle of the street daily for cooking fuel and warmth, I, too, have found myself skeptical about going to Guatemala for sohcker.

In France in 1998, getting your hands on match tickets was something of a nightmare. You see, just because you get a press credential doesn't mean you can get into the games— the media must also, like the fans, get individual tickets.* You had to line up in hot, crowded centers with two thousand of your colleagues and competitors and sulk until some word that resembled something close to "ticket" sounded over the microphone, at which point you all pushed forward in a giant scrum, hoping to get some plastic in your hands. If you are smart—or have been on the wrong end of one of these pile-ons—you learn to scope out a defensible point from which to charge to get your entry pass. I always try to have something right behind me, like a pillar or a few chairs, which I hope will delay the Brazilian media just long enough for me to get somewhere near the front of the line.

I realize these precautions sound insane, but most of you have never been around the seething gaggle that is the international soccer press—a large, foul-smelling, crumb- and nicotine-stained mass with a weakness for freebies and a perverse pleasure in seeing others suffer. I am excluding from this description the Brazilian media, which is a horror like no other. In Miami, at a post-Olympic press conference with the Brazilian coach Mario Zagallo, I made the mistake of asking a sweet old lady volunteer for a bag for my collection of press releases and notebooks. The sound of a plastic bag rubbing against nylon was like a mating call. Within two minutes (maybe less) Zagallo found himself explaining his team's embarrassing performance against Nigeria to an empty room;

---

*These tickets are free in the sense that there is no charge for them, but they are not easy to get.

the Brazilians had descended like a pack of raptors and all you could see of the old lady was a shock of white hair and bags flying into the crowd.

In Germany, however, everything was charming and swift. Bright, smiling blond teens whisked you from hello to ID check to photo to laminate to tiny bag to out the door with such speed I thought something had gone badly wrong. Even when I went back in to double-check that, yes, this was all you needed, just scan here, see it works, and out the door, the whole thing took less than ten minutes. This was almost *disappointingly* brief. We in the stunned press corps suddenly found ourselves with a whole afternoon to get into trouble.

The only things the German organizers couldn't control were the fans and the weather. And guess what? Right: the weather.

The England vs. Paraguay game had marked the start of a prolonged and widespread heat wave that swept inexorably from south to north. TV people began to complain about substandard pictures caused by the shadows from the stadium roofs, and despite the stifling conditions inside, some roofs were closed, turning the arenas into sweat lodges. Lodging that had seemed chilly became oppressive, and you faced a difficult choice each night: open the windows to the horns and yells outside, or close 'em up and slowly suffocate. My apartment had two bedrooms, and some nights I would haul myself up and trudge down the hall to see whether the air in the other room was moving a bit swifter and if the sheets were just that much cooler. One night I slept on the steel grille of the balcony, in hopes of finding one thing about Munich that was both cool and nonalcoholic. I had thought I would be avoiding the furnace of urban Chicago; instead it accompanied me.

With the heat came an explosion of yellow cards, for obvious reasons. When a team is tired out and sluggish, sometimes the only way to break up a play is to foul. Unfortunately, as referees were under orders from FIFA to clamp down on these tactics, more cards were doled out in the first round of the Cup than ever before. The heat also required more care on the part of the trainers, because dehydration is a serious problem in hot conditions, and players can lose alarming amounts of weight and water. Refs began to allow small "time-outs" for players to drink water on the sidelines, which further slowed the pace of the games. We had all made fun of David Beckham for complaining about the weather after the Paraguay match, but now I grasped that the British were well ahead of the curve.

England's second game, on June 15, was against Trinidad and Tobago, a tabloid hack's wet dream. The stories wrote themselves: Could the colony hold up against the former empire? Could goalkeeper (and West Ham washout) "Shaky" Shaka Hislop withstand Wayne Rooney? And how could Coach Eriksson's squeeze Nancy Dell'Olio and the WAGs' grim indifference to the Cup possibly compete against the combined booty power of a thousand Trinidadian women dancing for joy at every pass, feint, and even errant cross?

In Nuremberg, Trinidad and Tobago team members played the game of their lives against Britannia, and, until the eightieth minute, England's fans were unusually quiet and incredibly tense. One guy next to me at the Fan Fest was actually consuming his St. George's Cross flag, slowly sucking it in bit by bit, as though internalizing this symbol would help the lads to turn it on. (Instead he started coughing horribly.) England's heroes had deserted it. Striker Michael Owen looked as though his springs were out of tune, and Rooney was noticeably slower. "We're awful," England's fans moaned, mournfully watching what was possibly the entire population of Tobago shimmying in the aisles of the Frankenstadion.

And then, in the eighty-third minute, Peter Crouch, the six-foot-seven striker, hit home a header to give the English a win and a berth in the next round. Hislop's shoulders slumped. He had stopped twenty-one shots, only to let the twenty-second in. Outside the stadium, red-faced and shirtless England fans, swollen by sun and lager, queued up by the telephones, patiently waiting to call home.

"Mum!" shouted one teenager, bare-chested and wearing the St. George flag. "We won!"*

Across the country in Hamburg, Ecuador was busy beating up on Costa Rica. Ecuador's Iván Kaviedes, a player who had promised great things and transferred to England only to flop, proved his worth by scoring a key goal. He celebrated by whipping out a yellow Spider-Man mask—a tradition of his late teammate Otilino Tenorio, who was killed in a car crash in 2005—and racing around in blind glee like a child looking for a piñata.

These small moments emphasized how different this Cup was: What fans had seen were largely depressing, plodding games mercifully punctuated by fleeting, giddy moments. In

---

*Based on my observations at this Cup, I am forced to conclude England's fans may not understand what "live TV" is.

Germany, the celebrations were usually off the field. So, un-bowed despite the stifling conditions, the fans did the sensible thing: They began to drink. Amazingly, the combination of alcohol and heat didn't lead to the all-out mayhem it could have. However, there were moments.

The darker side of copious consumption had been seen the day before when Germany and Poland met. Taking pleasure before business, the German and Polish hooligans duked it out in the center of Dortmund in the Cup's first truly ugly event.

In Munich the night before, I had watched Croatian fans gamely attempt to samba to a makeshift Brazilian band, and tiny Japanese girls balance on the shoulders of large, unsteady Australian men. The camaraderie was honest and infectious. But in Dortmund the atmosphere was strikingly different. I felt the tension as soon as I stepped off the train. Polish and German fans did not mingle. Instead, the two camps carved out their spaces and glared at each other across the cobble-stones. This did not feel like a good time to make friends, much less interview anyone.

The police presence in Dortmund was larger than any-where else. Thousands were called out to keep the two historic enemies apart, and the cops had their hands full by four o'clock as drink and heat proved a combustible mix. Appar-ently, the cops moved in to confront a number of known Polish hooligans after receiving complaints of them harassing passersby. That operation went smoothly enough, with the al-leged hooligans submitting peacefully (if loudly) to the cops. But while the police were occupied with the Poles, German fans began to mass. Suddenly shaved-headed, bare-chested men were hurling chairs and bottles, and the ground was soon covered in glass. The cops moved in, forming human walls between fan groups, and though no one had been seriously injured, by the time it had all calmed down around nine P.M., close to five hundred people had been arrested.

That night the mood was somber. The Poles needed to win the game to stay in the Cup; the Germans needed a win to show their countrymen they were the real deal. Fifty thousand people were packed into the mile-long Fan Fest, stretching from the train station into the center of the city. Oddly, the side streets remained quiet; every once in a while a fan stumbled in to take a piss, but the only sounds that snapped the quiet were the howls of anguish as yet another German chance went awry. And there were plenty of those: The Poles were by far the more dynamic of the two sides on the night, rebounding well from their bad 2–0 loss to Ecuador five days earlier. It took a last-minute goal from sub Oliver Neuville for Germany to win the game, and it is worth noting that the Poles played the final twenty minutes (counting stoppage) with ten men after Radoslav Soboloveski was ejected for a second hard foul.

That night I filed my copy to the Web from Dortmund's train station café. Crouched over my laptop, using a makeshift cell-phone connection that was two parts duct tape and one part phone card, I thought about the old black rubber "couplers" that screwed onto phones for early transatlantic transmissions, and how I once had to bribe a store owner to use his credit card line to transmit twelve kilobytes worth of copy. Now I could send megabytes of info—pictures, video, audio—into the air. In twenty seconds, my story would be posted online to be read by some fourteen million people. Ten years ago, this would have been indistinguishable from magic. And yet, while I could do this, two groups of people with one game in common couldn't get along for five hours. The simplest connections seem to be the most elusive.

Because we were now midway through the first round of the Cup, I found my apartment increasingly being used as a way station for weary journalists and travelers. Every morning I'd wake up after another miserably truncated night's sleep and step over the bodies in my living room and the piles of laundry in search of what passed for coffee. Given my difficulties with German pharmacies, I looked awful at this point, with bruises under my eyes, a consumptive pallor, and cold sweats. I was still going, but it was getting tougher and tougher.

Ill health prevented me from going to several games. On June 16, lying frustrated and sweating on my couch, I saw Argentina's 6–1 rout of Serbia and Montenegro, and the debut of Lionel Messi. Even without me, attendance at the Cup passed the million-fan mark after only nine days and showed no sign of letting up. Also on June 16, Holland locked up its slot in the second round with a gritty win over Côte d'Ivoire (Ivory Coast),* possibly the best team in the Cup not to make it out of the group stage. The side led by Chelsea's Didier Drogba had the bad luck to be grouped with two Cup title contenders (Argentina and Holland), and Serbia and Montenegro was no slouch, either, despite being hammered by the Argentines.

---

*Fun fact: Côte d'Ivoire has maintained for years that there is, in fact, no translation for the name "Côte d'Ivoire" and that all of us who refer to the nation as Ivory Coast are incorrect. This is one of the (many) reasons that the country's FIFA code is "CIV." This has not stopped Côte d'Ivoire from referring to the USA as "Les Etats Unis," however.

But the next "big game," at least as far as the American audience was concerned, was on June 17 in Kaiserslautern, and I would be there. Since the USA had lost to the Czechs, the Americans needed a result (a tie or a win) against Italy to have any chance of getting to the next round. This was a tall order, and the Americans knew it. Escaping the population and an increasingly wrathful media, Team USA holed up at Ramstein Air Base in Kaiserslautern as a guest of the American military. There the players were surrounded by the things they missed from home (including cereal, according to midfielder Bobby Convey), leading a number of us pundits to wonder just how sheltered these kids truly were. Meanwhile, Arena was still trying to quash the firestorm that had erupted after the team's first outing.

The stadium in Kaiserslautern sits atop a steep hill and overlooks a fairly drab little town of one hundred thousand people. Neither the city nor its history is remarkable. It was named after the Holy Roman Emperor Frederick Barbarossa's favorite hunting grounds, the "Lautern"* (a stream that once ran through the older section of the city). General Omar Bradley took the city in the final days of World War II and since then it has maintained a multinational military presence. The majority of the military personnel (about thirty thousand) are American soldiers, making Kaiserslautern the home of the largest American troop concentration in Europe.[†]

---

*Fun fact: Frederick died crossing the Saleph River, apparently drowning in hip-deep water! Oh, the irony.

[†]Many of the American military personnel in Kaiserslautern, who would have been among the team's strongest supporters, were not able to attend the game: They didn't have tickets.

I didn't expect much from the match, to be truthful. The USA had never performed well in any meaningful match on European soil (and had performed very badly in meaningless matches as well) and the train ride in from Munich felt funereal. While the city was full of joy, American fans had the sense that this day could—and perhaps would—be the end of the line.

A few acquaintances and I arrived early in the city, and watched the first game of the day on a big-screen TV in a dingy bar. It was a shocker: Playing in Cologne, Ghana routed a tired Czech team 2–0, to throw their group wide open. Defender John Pantsil scored a key goal that had sociopolitical ramifications as well: Pantsil, who plays for the Israeli team Hapoel Tel Aviv, pulled an Israeli flag out of his shorts after scoring. He was promptly vilified by the world's Arab press. One paper, arguably the least vicious of the bunch, bizarrely suggested the player was an agent of the Mossad. The next day Ghana's football association would rebuke Pantsil, who was forced to apologize simply for saluting his club's fans who had traveled to see the game.

By the time kickoff for the game at Fritz-Walter Stadion rolled around, the streets of K-Town were crowded with Italian and American fans streaming up the center drag, up the hill, and into what was truly an overheated cauldron of a stadium. Possibly the biggest pro-USA crowd ever at an away match had turned out to see the game, and they would get their money's worth.

From the opening kickoff in Kaiserslautern, the Americans demonstrated the passion and flair that had been absent in their debut, running hard at a team they were not supposed to be able to beat. First came Clint Dempsey, looking more like a basketball player than a midfielder with his shuffle steps, powering the ball into—and sometimes off players and through—the box. Then came Convey on the other flank, putting crosses and corners alike on their heads. Up the middle ran Donovan with Claudio Reyna tailing behind.

At first the Italians seemed amused. Then the smiles of Fabio Cannavaro and Francesco Totti grew wan and taut. The Americans were not rolling over, and were not stopping. Ten minutes passed. Then twenty.

Even when Alberto Gilardino seized the lead for Italy in the twenty-second minute by converting a spectacular free kick after Andrea Pirlo was felled by the USA's Pablo Mastroeni too close to his team's box, the USA grabbed the ball and swiftly restarted, to rush at keeper Gianluigi Buffon again. Five minutes later, off a Convey cross, Cristian Zaccardo headed the ball into his own net under heavy pressure from Carlos Bocanegra.

Disaster struck for Italy just before the end of the first half when Daniele de Rossi was ejected for deliberately elbowing Brian McBride in the face, leaving the lanky forward soaked in his own blood. But three minutes later Mastroeni was tossed, too, when he spiked Pirlo, seemingly in retaliation.

After the break things hit the skids quickly for the Yanks when Eddie Pope was ejected following a second, stupid foul. The ejection gave the Italians a chance, and to the Americans' credit they did not bend. It wasn't for Italy's want of trying, either: Kasey Keller robbed Alessandro Del Piero point-blank in the seventy-second minute and Gennaro Gattuso in the seventy-ninth. Vincenzo Iaquinta spearheaded a late resurgence of the *Azzurri* that gave the Americans fits for the last ten minutes.

Finishing with just nine men, the USA managed a 1–1

draw. It was the first positive result in Europe in a major game for the USA, and the players celebrated, justifiably, as though they had won.

Outside the Fritz-Walter arena, joyous Americans crammed the streets from the stadium to the railway, making the city a sea of red and white from noon until well past midnight. Leaning out of pub windows and sitting at roadside cafés, American fans exulted in a result that kept them alive in the tournament, but also mourned what might have been. The Americans had dominated the match, erasing the memory of their tepid start four days earlier against the Czechs.

"Not many teams would have held their composure under a situation like that," said Arena at a postgame press conference. "The USA deserves to be proud tonight."

When asked whether he saw the result as a restoration of his reputation, Arena demurred, saying the credit went to his team, even noting that the much-maligned DaMarcus Beasley was "spectacular" as a sub.

With Ghana's 2–0 win over the Czech Republic in that earlier group match, the USA was left on the bottom of Group E and with inferior goal difference going into what was now a final, winner-take-all game against Ghana. But the result against Italy gave the Americans something they didn't have before kickoff: a chance.

"The guys showed a lot of heart today. We're alive, and who knows what can happen," said Keller. "With four points we might be able to get out of the group. We're going to give it our best shot."

The USA has unfortunately shown over the years that they can be world-beaters one day and sops the next. Certainly the team that played Italy looked completely different from the team that lost to the Czechs. That inconsistency was something even the hyperprepared Arena had not been able to eliminate.

And to get into the knockout stage, the USA would still have to do one thing the Americans hadn't yet managed to do on their own—score a goal.

The train ride home from K-Town was oversold, with bodies sprawled across the aisles, tables, benches, and jump seats. The conductors tried to check tickets at first, but quickly gave up after it became clear the carriages were impassable. For four hours the train hurtled through the black German night in silence. I got a text message from my wife, Li, about the happiest man in Germany: The lone Ghanaian fan left in Munich was paraded around the Marienplatz on the backs of Australian and Brazilian supporters.

I thought about Italy's coach, Marcelo Lippi, and the bluster of excuses he'd given at his own press briefing. (Listening to him, you would have thought his team had fallen victim to the worst chain of circumstances ever.) I thought about Clint Dempsey, who had desperately wanted to do something to help, and had. I thought about the people around me, and it occurred to me that the greatest characteristic of the hard-core fan might well be the willingness to put up with unbelievable hardship just to see two hours of entertainment.

When the train pulled into Munich, the sun was beginning to peek up over the town hall. Fans coming off the trains were met by those setting out for the next game. The French were playing South Korea in Leipzig, and the Aussies and the Brazilians were streaming into Munich.

The Brazil–Australia game on June 18 was the hottest ticket in Munich. The Aussies wanted to play the Brazilians, and both sets of fans were out in force—energetic, good-humored, and on the hustle something fierce. A number of Brazilian fans came and quite literally danced for their suppers; every few blocks you could find a small entrepreneurial group demonstrating *capoeira*, the dance-infused martial art, inside a tight ring of tourists.

These demos were magnets for the Japanese fans, who snaked their way through the Munich market in a relentless quest to take as many photos as possible. As I tried to make my way to the subway for the game, small waves of Japanese tourists were coursing from one *capoeira* circle to the next, and it was easy to be swept away by their enthusiasm. When the gent in front of me stopped to take a picture of the backs of people's heads, I found myself actually weighing his choice of subject instead of cursing.

Unlike their neighbors the South Koreans (who bizarrely believed their team could win the Cup), the Japanese fans generally had a more somber, reflective approach. "We just hope the team does not embarrass the country," a man named Ken told me over a beer that morning.

This was perhaps the most devastating commentary possible on a team. Japan was still smarting from having given up three goals to the Aussies in the final six minutes of their opening match,* which pretty much took them out of contention before they'd had a chance to get going. In contrast, the win energized the Aussies, who now had a legitimate shot

---

*John Aloisi nabbed the third in stoppage time after Tim Cahill had pounded in goals in the eighty-fourth and eighty-ninth minutes. Aloisi's goal came three minutes after that, but since the clock in football stops at ninety, this was *officially* a six-minute span. It's not like conceding three goals in eight minutes is any better.

at getting past the Asian champs and into the second round if they grabbed one point from their final two first-round games.

This state of affairs had put most Australian visitors in Bavaria into a grand mood, and at the time Ken and I were watching three drunken teens being hoisted far up above the roof of the Viktualienmarkt by a crane. It was damn early for that sort of thing, but it was also quite early to be drinking. "You don't want to stand there," Ken said, pointing to some suspicious splashes on the ground.

Ridiculous, well-meaning, and grabby (if you were a woman), the Australians had made it clear from the start they were there to party and nothing was going to get in their way. Case in point: An Australian marching band traveled from Queensland to serenade their side against Brazil, and oompahed their way across Munich until dawn for a full *five days* before the game, a performance that had my landlord begging someone to steal that damn tuba.

On match day Li and I were hanging out with three Scottish fans from Dundee,* sharing a love for all things Tayside (you know, it's never cold in a pub in Dundee). The three guys were longtime friends who had taken a great many holidays together. Two of them had the good fortune to find a hotel, but the third was camping out and had lost his tent stakes, which confused him. "Why in the world would anyone steal my hitch and stakes, and leave my tent?" he asked. Four hours

---

*I spent a great deal of time in Scotland and am an ardent Dundee United fan. Arsenal, however, is my family's club, my wife, my father, and I having followed the club's exploits for years. For the record, my mother, ever the contrarian, is a Manchester United fan, which causes no end of strife.

before kickoff, we decided to split into two groups: Half of us were going to the game (I was the only one with a ticket) and the other half were going to see the atmosphere around the Allianz Arena and then head to the Fan Fest.

Unfortunately, so many people were trying to get to the Allianz that police were only letting those who swore up and down they weren't going anywhere near the stadium board the trains; it was only after much discussion and waving of my credential that I persuaded a cop even to let me remain on the platform. This meant a change in plans: Li would go off with our new pals, and I'd head to the Allianz alone.[*]

At the same time, a minor scandal had broken out involving the Socceroos: Sky Sports reported that members of the team were betting on the games, which would violate FIFA rules. Backup keeper Željko Kalac was the bookie; the players had bet on which one of them would be the first to score a goal at the Cup.[†] FIFA subsequently decided its rules only prohibited betting with professional bookmakers, not bets among teammates,[‡] but the incident cast a small cloud of doubt over the upcoming match.

---

[*]Li says: "If you're going to wander off with groups of strange men, make sure they are Scottish. They are always polite."

[†]Tim Cahill was the runaway favorite, and indeed he was the first Aussie ever to score a goal in the Cup finals.

[‡]FIFA's attitude surprised many observers, as intrasquad gambling has been a serious problem for some teams. One example: High-stakes gambling has been blamed for causing deep fissures at West Ham in England's Premier League. On March 4, 2007, the London *Observer* reported that as much as $100,000 was being lost per sitting in card games, quoting an unidentified player as saying: "I've never seen anything like it in my career. It's one big mess here." The story went on to allege that three members of the team were in or seeking counseling for gambling addiction.

It turned out there was no need to worry: The game was brilliant. Australia controlled the flow of the play for long stretches and gave the world champs all they could handle in a gritty performance that raised more doubts about the form of Brazil's attackers Ronaldo and Ronaldinho, the latter in particular having been accused of being out of shape. Journeymen players such as Harry Kewell and Jason Culina were elevated into Aussie heroes.

The rest of my group, locked out of the Fan Fest and the Allianz Arena and looking for a place to see the game, were turned away from one beer garden after the next due to over-crowding. They finally ended up at an upscale restaurant that had been entirely taken over by Brazilian and Australian fans, some lined up ten deep at the bar. The lone waiter on call, a very blond, very effeminate man named Mario, quickly gave up on taking orders and began sending busboys around with large platters of beer in mugs.

There was no chance of hearing the match, as the Australian fans kept up a steady, good-natured patter that ultimately degenerated into long, off-key renditions of "Waltzing Matilda." At any one time, two or three competing versions of the song were going back and forth within a crowd that fifteen minutes into the game had spilled out the open windows and over the railings to block the road outside.

Men dressed in kangaroo outfits were leaping on tables, leading the room in ever-wobblier renditions, and one Aussie fan got a big cheer when he managed to get a Brazilian girl to give him her bikini top, decorated in the green and yellow flag, in exchange for a little bit of hush. She leaned over, top-less, to say to the group, "What a depressing song. Oh god, if they lose I will have to hear it all night." The Aussie cheerfully donned his souvenir and wore it for the rest of the evening.

Even Mario's attempts at Germanic efficiency broke down a half hour in, though, when some patrons decided to have sustenance with their alcohol. The waiter was forced to issue a moratorium on food orders until halftime. The busboys began bringing out minikegs of beer, and people started passing those back along with pint glasses full of broken-up pretzels.

Back at the game, Adriano finally broke the deadlock after the half with a low, grass-cutting shot from just outside the penalty area that slid past Australian keeper Mark Schwarzer and inside the near post. The goal sparked furious celebrations inside the arena and out; players jumped off the bench to surround Adriano on the sideline, where the entire team performed a celebratory dance known as "rocking the baby," a sort of stationary frug, while the Aussies looked on unamused. Adriano kissed his hands and pointed up—a gesture he makes in memory of his late father every time he scores—and the game was won.

At the restaurant, the festive mood had not dimmed. But with ten minutes to go in the game, Mario, out of nowhere, cried out: "WE HAVE RUN OUT OF BEER!" There was an uncomfortable pause as three burly Aussies approached him. In one swoop, the Aussies hoisted Mario on their shoulders, and the restaurant exploded into cheers of, "Mario! Mario!" as the pale and sweating waiter was paraded through the restaurant as a hero. The fans had drunk the place dry. Few there noticed when Brazil's Fred scored the capper in the ninetieth minute. The Aussies had both won and lost.

A woman from South Africa proclaimed, "Our World Cup will *not* run out of beer."

"Most days you're lucky if you don't run out of water down there!" one of her friends reminded her.

The day devolved into ebullient celebration. One of the Scottish gents went off to take a nap in the sun; the rest headed back for the center market and more lager.

DOWN AND DIRTY

The most intense and concentrated phase of the World Cup kicked off on June 20 with the start of the "four-a-days." As you might guess, this meant four games a day as the first round wound down. This was the sprint before the "real" Cup began.

We began with Germany, Ecuador, and England having already locked up their second-round slots in Groups A and B, leaving Sweden and Trinidad and Tobago battling for the final slot. The result was something of a day off for German fans, who watched their Mannschaft beat Ecuador handily, 3–0, in a game without consequence. It was just another day to party,* and the teens and those old enough to know better jammed the cities.

---

*I can say this: The Germans may be micromanaging, unspontaneous weirdos, but they know how to throw a good party. Based on my observations of the beer gardens, the stages of German excitement are: polite; quiet; quiet; quiet; on the table, shirt off, whoopin' and a-hollerin'; brutally hungover. Even when there were few stars on the field, there were plenty in the streets.

Up on the crane above the market (now in near-constant use) one of the teens took off her top, revealing a torso streaked in the yellow, red, and black of the German flag, cheering the hearts of all men below her. Body paint was a big thing this Cup: It was lightweight, practical, and, on women, helped sell more copies of *Bild* than even those pictures of Sweden's female fans smooching.

Sweden's female fans—as photographed by German magazines—seemed always to be locked in passionate embraces, oblivious to the action on the field. Then again, since most of that action involved their star, Freddie Ljungberg, getting into fights with his teammates, perhaps they knew something I didn't. Whatever the reason, Sweden locked up the last second-round slot with a dull draw with England as Trinidad and Tobago fought to a valiant 2–2 draw with Paraguay. Liplocks covered the front pages the next day.

Storms rolled into Munich the following afternoon, creating monsoon conditions for the Ivory Coast vs. Serbia and Montenegro match. Ivory Coast had already been eliminated from the Cup—though considered one of the bright spots of the tournament, it lost its first two games—and its opponent didn't even exist anymore as one nation; FIFA had to warn the Serbia and Montenegro team to show up for its final game. I went to it because I wanted to see if these two countries would put on a show, and how the crowd would react to a match that was, to American sensibilities, meaningless.

Oddly enough, the people who showed up wearing Ivory Coast's colors were almost exclusively white—TV cameramen at the match had to search for black fans to put on the air. Why? German customs officials denied many Africans access to the country despite the World Cup being quite happy to take fans' money when they tried to buy tickets. Germany (like many other countries we're familiar with) apparently has an immigration "problem," and it was thought the black Africans would stay. So the promised visas never materialized, and many African fans were left home.

This was a huge loss for the Cup, because African fans have a great tradition of supporting their teams. Also, I was informed, without them the witchcraft the medicine men were practicing would be far less potent. Nonetheless, potions were being flung—one sorcerer was trying to get his pouches onto the field near the Serbian goalpost when security stopped him—and two gentlemen in elaborate (and I assume authentic) tribal getups spent the entire game on their feet, casting spells and warding off hexes.

Ivory Coast also got aid and comfort from the crowd of Croatian fans who crashed the match, wearing their own country's football strip or its basketball jerseys topped with Ivory Coast's caps. When the Serbian national anthem was played, these fans whistled loudly in an attempt to drown it out.

On the other hand, the Serbians (the fans never once chanted or even whispered the word "Montenegro") were a surly bunch. I rode in with them on the train and the atmosphere was extremely tense. I soon found out why: There was a significant far-right presence at the game and a number of white "iron" cross flags were smuggled in and flown.

The game was not a pretty performance. The Serbs fouled, pushed, and cursed their way through the ninety minutes in an ill and downright reckless temper. Ivory Coast's coach, Henri Michel, told journalists before the match that he thought his team's failures in the tournament were due to defensive lapses. That was in evidence on Serbia's first goal:

Dejan Stankovic lofted the ball into Nikola Žigić, who ran in with only a sprawled Boubacar Barry to beat. On the second, Saša Ilic beat both keeper Barry and Cyrille Domoraud, primarily because he was left open in the box.

Ivory Coast then won a penalty kick when Milan Dudic was caught for a hand ball in the box. The air began to crackle with static electricity and a deafening peal of thunder ripped above the Allianz just before Aruna Dindane sank the team's first goal, from the spot. Just five minutes later, Albert Nadj was ejected for a second hard foul. The Serbs would finish with ten men. It seemed whatever was in those medicine sachets was working.

After the break, it was all Ivory Coast. The rain was just pouring down—the ball stopping and skipping as it hit puddles on the pitch, the vaunted Allianz's drainage system completely overloaded. But Ivory Coast looked fast and sharp. Dindane headed one home to level the match and the Coast's small passel of fans were elated. Unbelievably, with four minutes left, Dudic did it again—blocking a shot from Bonaventure Kalou with his hand to set up a penalty kick attempt that could win Ivory Coast its first-ever World Cup game.

All but one set of eyes were locked on the south end of the pitch. Boubacar Barry couldn't watch. He turned his back to the field, kneeled in the mud, and prayed against his goalpost. The rain was washing down his face, and you could see his torso shaking as Serbia's fans taunted him. His eyes were closed so tightly, and his face and jaw were so tense, I thought he was going to tear something—this was one of those few rare moments in sport when it is clear that an experienced athlete is, for once, completely aware of and immersed in the crowd. With each shout and each moment his face grew paler, and still he did not look and did not stop praying.

Then the crowd erupted. Barry nervously glanced up and saw the Serbians were looking away, disgusted. Kalou had scored. Barry let out a scream of joy you could hear in the upper deck, got up, and ran from his goal toward his teammates on the sidelines. The Elephants had won, and, as though on cue, the rain stopped.

That night, tens of thousands of us rushed the gates at the U-Bahn stop—the Munich police had tried to shut the subways down on schedule and had not provided enough cars to get the fans away from the Allianz. Pushing and shoving broke out, and a small melee emerged before a frightened ticket lady flung the gate back up, sending us rushing onto the platform below. Despite the trains being full and ready to go, the conductors waited for eleven minutes before taking off, driving the drunk, overheated, sopping-wet fans crazy. What could we do? We steamed in the closed cars until, at long last, they pulled out and headed back to the city.

The USA's final first-round appearance was in Nuremberg, a must-win game in a compact stadium in a compact city, staged just two hundred yards from the infamous rally grounds of the Nazi regime.

Nuremberg has a long pedigree: It was the "unofficial" center of the Holy Roman Empire, home to Albrecht Dürer, and, more recently, the symbol of "authentic Germany" for the Nazi Party in the late 1920s and early 1930s. If Munich was the capital of the Nazi regime, Nuremberg was arguably the movement's spiritual home. The vicious anti-Semite Julius

Streicher lived here, in part because the city had expelled its Jewish population some four hundred years earlier, in 1499. Nuremberg was profoundly unlike other major cities in Europe in layout, architecture, and attitude. English poet Philip Larkin once wrote that Nuremberg embodied "the architecture of the age, [and] its heroes, the working class,"* a judgment that neatly sums up the image of the city the Nazis wished to project to the world at large.† The availability of land on which to stage their rallies allowed the Nazis to transform Nuremberg into a museum piece backdrop for their propaganda machine. Nuremberg was also an important production center for the Axis, with slave labor turning out war matériel.

The city was destroyed in 1945 by Allied bombers: On January 2, almost the entire ancient center of the city was leveled in one hour. What remains today has largely been reconstructed from its ruins. The aftermath of this campaign was immortalized in W. H. Auden's "Memorial for the City,"‡ a work based explicitly on the poet's service with the U.S. Air Force's Strategic Bombing Survey. Said Auden of the time: "We asked them if they minded being bombed . . . We got no answers that we did not expect."§

---

*The piece I am quoting from comes from Larkin's *Further Requirements*, a collection of essays, reviews, and oddments that was published posthumously by Faber and Faber in 2001.
†I mention Larkin because it's worth noting that not all Nazis were German. Larkin's father, Sydney, was a Fascist, and Larkin himself was spectacularly racist and right wing. The Nazi regime enjoyed a great deal of sympathy in some quarters of England at the time.
‡"Where our past is a chaos of graves and the barbed wire stretches ahead / into our future until it is lost to sight."
§This is quoted in Cornelia Pearsall's "The Poet and the Postwar City," *Raritan Quarterly* 17, no. 2, Rutgers Press.

Postwar, Nuremberg was chosen for symbolic reasons as the site of the Nazi war-crimes trials in which Hermann Goering and twenty-three others were judged. Since that time, Nuremberg has attempted to rebuild itself as a modern "city of peace and human rights."

To get into the stadium, you had to pass the rally grounds, now empty and somewhat overgrown but still capable of conveying how awe-inspiring and encompassing those rallies must have been. The grounds seem to go on for miles, and while the swastikas have long since been dynamited off the edifices, an unsettling power remains—especially after weeks of watching gleeful crowds chant national slogans. While I hate to admit it, there is a seductive quality about the place to this day: It must have been thrilling for people to lose themselves in so vast a space, and, for good or for ill, become part of a giant collective.

American fans were not particularly welcome in Nuremberg. Obviously some of the anger at Americans was political, caused by a war in Iraq that many Europeans (and Americans) saw as immoral and illegal. Some hackles were further raised by Team USA's unthinking naïveté: A (perhaps overly) sensitive European press criticized the Americans for their use of war metaphors to describe their efforts. To wit, Arena had described McBride as a "warrior" before the Ghana game and Eddie Johnson had unfortunately carried on in detail about the team's games being a "war." (This was yet another sign of culture gap; the players were taking a page from American football, but the fact that twenty-four fouls were called on the Americans in the USA–Italy game stoked some powder.) On game day a significant group of Germans had come out to cause trouble in the guise of supporting Ghana (some of these "fans" having passionately argued against allowing genuine African fans into the country). Scuffles broke out in the crowd, at the train platform, and outside the stadium, and I was involved; someone decked my wife and another spat at her. It was not a pleasant afternoon out, and the fact that all this took place in the shadow of the rally grounds gave everything a sour feel.

Missing for the game for the USA were defender Eddie Pope (two yellows, against Italy) and midfielder Pablo Mastroeni (a straight red, ditto). But Ghana was also missing a pair of key players: Asamoah Gyan and Sulley Muntari, who both scored in the Black Stars' 2–0 win over the Czechs, had been suspended for accumulation of cards. So the USA felt it had, at least, a chance.

It was a tough game from the whistle. Eddie Lewis got caught above the eye mere minutes in, with John Mensah delivering an elbow. And the USA's chances dimmed in the twenty-first minute when Claudio Reyna made a fatal—and painful—mistake. Reyna momentarily dithered with the ball in the back third of the field, seemingly at a loss for what to do. Haminu Dramani made him pay for it, crashing through him with a hard challenge that sent the captain down to the ground with his knee in agony and then going in alone against Keller to score. Reyna limped off the field, finished for the tournament.

The Americans grabbed one back two minutes before halftime when Dempsey was sprung by DaMarcus Beasley, who took the ball off the foot of Derek Boateng and sent it cutting toward the Ghanaian goal. Dempsey one-timed it to the back of the net for a small moment of glory for the USA. Celebrating with a small jig, he was mobbed by his teammates at the corner flag.

Two minutes later, one of the more controversial decisions of the Cup was made when German ref Markus Merk awarded a penalty to Ghana for what he judged to be a foul on Razak Pimpong by Oguchi Onyewu. Onyewu, who has a reputation for roughness, had won a ball in the air cleanly, but Pimpong had dropped to the turf as though shot. Stephen Appiah sunk the penalty easily and that was it.

This call had implications beyond the game, as Merk, who is considered one of the best refs in the world, would not officiate another match. FIFA does not publicly criticize its officials, but it was clear to longtime observers that the refereeing committee felt he had blown the call. The incident also put the lie to the talk of how new technology would change the sport. Officials in soccer have more influence than referees in any other sport, and yet because of the size of the field, even the best referee will always miss things.

On the play, Merk was downfield, viewing the incident from behind the players. From that angle, it looked indeed as though Onyewu had fouled Pimpong. But replays from the sidelines, where the linesman was, showed no foul. The big question is why the linesman—who could have contacted Merk via his headset—didn't bail the ref out. Here, the culture of officiating is partly to blame (refs traditionally loathe being "helped" by their assistants) but one has to wonder what those headsets are for if no one is going to use them.

Merk was not the only ref to get caught out despite the new technology. Graham Poll, the English ref, gave three yellow cards to Croatian Josip Simunic and missed the fact that a key goal scored by the Australian Harry Kewell came from an offside position. In neither case did Poll's assistants help him, and he, too, was subsequently relieved of his whistle.

Onyewu, though, should never have had to make the play in question. Carlos Bocanegra had, bizarrely, crossed the ball to him, forcing Onyewu to make a play. Had Bocanegra just put the ball out of bounds—as a defender is supposed to do—the situation would never have arisen. Bocanegra's play was an illustration of how naive American players can sometimes be: In trying to do the impossible, to turn nothing into something, Bocanegra helped doom his side. Later, Landon Donovan got free with about ten minutes left, but rather than shooting on net, he passed the ball. That one moment summed up the afternoon for a team that had the will but had lost its way.

Tens of thousands of American fans had attended the World Cup in person, a first. These were not hard-core soccer fans, nor eccentrics, nor backpackers crossing Europe who stumbled upon the tournament. These were sports fans. They may have come to see a curiosity, but they came away with the bitter, firsthand knowledge of both how harsh and how poetic the game can be. Those fans remained in their seats in Nuremberg long after the game had ended, holding flags, looking glumly down at their laps.

"Unfortunately, they [Team USA] have to go home, but they also deserve to be in the final sixteen," said Ghana coach Ratomir Dujkovic. This was magnanimous given that, according to some players' complaints, Arena did not even shake his counterpart's hand after the game.

For Ghana, joining Italy in the second round was sweet vindication. The Black Stars had been the odd team out in one of the Cup's toughest groups, and in its first visit to the big stage managed to reduce teams FIFA ranked numbers two and five to chaff.

As for the American team, it headed home with many questions. What would be the fate of the mercurial Donovan, who looked dazzling against Italy and childish against all other comers? How could the Americans, even ignoring the inflated status FIFA imposed upon them, show such heart and yet disappoint so utterly? Why did some of the players chosen for the Cup not even suit up?

For the first time in America, those questions were asked in public. Once, a performance like Team USA's would have been greeted with apathy or resignation, or simply ignored. In 2006 it was greeted with anger.

Arena was unusually downbeat after the game. He looked like a man left holding a fistful of losing betting slips. The gambles he had made—bringing the players' wives, ignoring some overseas players and some younger home talent, and relying heavily on the same core that had played so well in 2002—had not paid off.

"These things happen," said Arena, glumly, as the fans trickled out. "They happen a lot to our team, but they happen. I thought we actually played pretty well."

Elsewhere that day, Australia qualified for the second round with a hard-fought 2–all draw against Croatia. Brazil sent Japan out with a 4–0 thumping. And the Czech Republic, which had lost Jan Koller to injury, looked tired out against a driven Italian side. The Czechs lost 2–0, and went home. The first round of the Cup would end with France vs. Togo.

The 2006 Cup had been a tough one for Togo. Togo's players went on strike immediately before the tournament started, demanding payment for their performance, due in three days' time. This is not unusual in African football, where players are sometimes not paid at all; teams from a variety of nations have staged such strikes before key tourneys in an attempt to embarrass their governments into cutting checks. However, it was the latest in a series of blows for the team. Its original coach, Stephen Keshi, was sacked after he and top player Emmanuel Adebayor were involved in a heated exchange in front of journalists. Adebayor, who is today a star forward at Arsenal, accused Keshi of attempting to insinuate himself as a player agent during transfer negotiations between Adebayor's then club Monaco and the London powers. The allegation was a serious one—which Keshi denied—but he got the chop. He was replaced by German Otto Pfister, who insisted it be written into his contract that the Togolese Federation would be kept at arm's length. But the firing did not sit well with many players, and the team arrived in Germany deeply divided.

Togo's players wanted $200,000 each to play in the tournament, plus $39,000 each per win and $20,000 per draw. The average yearly salary in the sub-Saharan country, heavily dependent on phosphate mining and coffee, is $400. When, on June 10, the situation had not been resolved, Pfister resigned, saying the team was too distracted. "For me, a dream has ended," he said in a statement. All hell broke loose. Pfister threatened to sue after a Togolese official said he was a traitorous drunk.

Other coaches told the Togolese Federation to get stuffed, and FIFA hit the roof. Never before had a team threatened to drop out of the World Cup at the last moment. According to FIFA spokesman Andreas Herren, FIFA executives met with the Togolese players, warning them, in his words, that: "If you don't travel [to the game], it could be the worst thing you could do." The team got on the plane to Frankfurt, and the word was FIFA had agreed to pay the players out of its own pocket, withholding the money from the $5.7 million owed each nation for making the tournament in the first place. (After the Cup, FIFA also withheld the Togo Federation's share of the profits, a severe punishment.)

Pfister showed up on the bench for Togo's first game, which it lost to South Korea, 2–1. The Swiss then crushed the Togolese, 2–0, in their June 19 game.

As for France, it has had a funny history with the sport of soccer. The World Cup was dreamed up there by Rimet, and the European Cup was built by the French sports newspaper *L'Equipe*. But for most of the twentieth century team sports (perhaps excepting cycling, though the individual racers were feted more than the *domestiques*) were viewed as somewhat déclassé. When the World Cup was staged in France in 1998, the population initially greeted the event with something between indifference and contempt. A French slang word sums up this attitude: *bof*, or "whatever." Had France not gone on to win the whole thing, I believe, in hindsight, the 1998 Cup would have had little to no lasting impact.

Today things are very different. There is an obvious pride in the sport and in the great French players, who rank among the best technical practitioners of the modern game. The French combine the grit and hard play of the country's second-most loved sport, rugby, with a finesse often attributed to the

Italians. There's also no getting around the quality of their league and teams: Lyon, Marseille, PSG, and Monaco are routinely among the best sides in Europe,* and while the league has struggled to retain the interest of a decidedly fickle public, the French can really play this game they helped make famous.†

Inside the stadium in Cologne, it was a tense evening for the thirty thousand French fans, all of whom expected the worst of the team. France, with all its talent, has been famously divided in recent years, and its coach, the astrology-consulting Raymond Domenech, was seen as a polarizing

---

*Arsenal is also one of France's best supported clubs. Its French-born coach, Arsène Wenger, made his name at Monaco, but has become a fixture in England for the gunner's graceful style, which at its best can truly be mesmerizing. Wenger, who resembles a grown-up Tintin, all pinch-faced and reedy with googly eyes that flare when something displeases him, is an ascetic whose hobby is said to be watching obscure third-division football matches in the quiet of his home. Arsenal enjoys fervent support across the Channel because it has been the home of a number of great modern French players. Its former captain is Thierry Henry, widely acknowledged as the best striker on the planet, and Patrick Vieira, France's captain, was for years the London club's midfielder anchor.

†If you wish to see how French football once was, hop over to Paris Saint-Germain's home ground, Parc des Princes. Where the Stade de France is plush and modern, Le Parc, the home of one of France's great football clubs—which is sponsored, in part, by the city itself!—is stark and run-down. This is not a new thing. When I saw games there in the 1970s, football was absolutely an outsider sport. In that era, PSG's fans were largely North African immigrants. How ignored was the sport? During the summer exhibition tournaments you could see teams that today would be lightning rods for trouble—Israeli sides such as Maccabi Tel Aviv, or top rivals such as Monaco—play before listless houses. And what was Parc des Princes's most famous moment? It perhaps came during the European Cup, when fans from England's Leeds rioted, ripping out the arena's seats and tossing them onto the pitch and each other. That's where the sport was. Parc des Princes is still home to a wicked crew of "ultra" fans, and they still cause problems.

figure. But Patrick Vieira, the gigantic French captain, celebrated his birthday on June 23 with a big gift to his country. Within six minutes, Vieira scored and assisted on the two critical goals against outsider Togo that took his staggering nation into the next round of the World Cup.

The French team, which was in dire straits until Vieira and the talismanic midfielder Zinedine Zidane agreed to return for one last shot at glory, managed in one night to erase the bitter memories of 2002. In South Korea, the team failed to score a goal and were out in the first round; here, they beat a former colony to reaffirm this was a Cup dominated by the old guard.

By the final whistle, *les bleus* were celebrating in the stands, and the impish Michel Platini, one of the nation's greatest players, could be seen in the upper loge mugging for the camera. Platini was sticking his tongue out as though to say "I told you so" to the entire world.

What did we learn from round one? Well, the best teams in the Cup to this date were the ones who most successfully camouflaged the fatigue of their top stars. It's worth noting that Holland's scorers—Arjen Robben of Chelsea, Ruud van Nistelrooy of Real Madrid, and Robin van Persie of Arsenal—all played on top teams but did not appear day after day for their clubs. It's also worth noting how out of sorts the stars who *did* play in virtually every game—the Frank Lampards, the Thierry Henrys—looked in the heat.

But it also has to be said how bad some of the teams in this edition of the tournament were. Arguably, between eight and sixteen sides could have been lopped off without anyone missing them. Is it solely the fault of Togo, Angola, Iran, Saudi

Arabia, or Japan (to pick a few) that their soccer is so poor? No. Like the United States, these teams were forced to play weak opponents to qualify and have few impact players getting big-league experience. Angola is perhaps the most egregious example: This is a team essentially fielding semipro players in the world's biggest sporting event. The salaries of the entire Angolan team barely approached the transfer fee for a *single* decent mid-level player.

The expanded tournament was intended to give more nations a shot at the brass ring and to encourage the improvement of their leagues and playing facilities. But it hasn't happened. The majors—CONMEBOL and UEFA—continue to dominate. If you speak with the folks in regional governments in the Asian, African, and North American federations, they all point to expanded regional and local tournaments for whatever improvements they have managed to make. It's not enough. Germany proved that there is still a wide gulf between the elite level and the ambitious, energetic countries trying to match it. Germany also showed that the minnows are better at playing not to lose than playing to win. There was little carefree about the sixteen sides who were sent home. That hurt, too.

THE SHORT-TIMERS
AND THE "REAL" CUP

Walking through the crowds to the Allianz Arena on the afternoon of June 24, I was confronted by a large man wearing moose horns. They were real horns, presumably from a real, albeit dead, moose. The man's neck looked as though it was about to snap from the weight, but since he was extremely drunk, he wasn't feeling the damage.

MooseMan was one of twenty thousand overheated Swedish fans who turned out for the game that kicked off the "real" World Cup—the Cup in which every game matters and teams must win to stay alive. There are no ties, no help, and, for some, no hope. The knockout phase is efficient and cruel, and lots of teams coast through the group stage only to be derailed here. This is also the stage of the World Cup where the teams that have saved a bit in their tanks are rewarded for their prudence. Gone were the slick, playful moves Argentina had used to toy with Serbia, while players who had looked a bit sapped in the heat—Brazil's Kaká, Ronaldo, and Ronaldinho come to mind—began to show they weren't really just going through the motions.

The match with Germany would make it a long day for the Swedes. The German side dispatched them in twelve minutes with two goals from Lukas Podolski, both set up by Miroslav Klose. The remaining seventy-eight minutes were an exercise in cruise control by the Germans, who now seemed destined to win the tournament on their home soil. It was, frankly, a tedious game.

The far better match was in Leipzig, where Mexico faced Argentina in a city overrun by men in sombreros. This was one of the first truly great games of the Cup—a wide-open contest that saw Mexico give the former world champion everything it could have wanted, and then some.

On paper, the game appeared to be a damp squib: Mexico had struggled to get out of its group—it was held to a goalless draw by Angola, after all!—and Argentina was the tourney favorite, especially after its spectacular, oft-viewed twenty-five-touch scoring sequence against Serbia and Montenegro.

But five minutes in, Rafael Marquez tucked in a Mario Méndez free kick to silence the crowd and give the Mexicans the lead. Argentina would equalize just five minutes later when Hernán Crespo ricocheted a shot off the head of Mexican forward Jared Borgetti, who'd been pushed back into a defensive role on the play.

Marquez is worth a side note: He is a rarity in Mexican soccer, a truly successful player with an overseas pedigree, gained from his long, ongoing stint at Barcelona. Mexican players are notoriously poor travelers, to the detriment of their national team. (Borgetti, in fact, would flame out at Bolton in England despite having all the talent in the world.) The last Mexican player who made it big overseas was Hugo

Sanchez,* but despite his undeniable grace, Sanchez never had the support to elevate the national team into a credible threat. Even in 1986, when Mexico hosted the Cup, its team was rightfully lightly regarded. Marquez has helped transform the Mexican team into something very different. Today, in large part because the players around Marquez have markedly improved (ironically, under increased pressure from rival the USA), the Mexicans are serious contenders.

What came next was an hour and a half of end-to-end football. Argentina, run by the great midfielder Juan Román Riquelme, tried to pick apart a tough Mexican offside trap, sending Crespo and compatriot Esteban Cambiasso on searching forays through toward Oswaldo Sanchez's goal. Riquelme, so gifted with the ball at his feet, drew the defenders forward to him using deceptively simple footwork: small rolls of the ball back with his cleats on top to force a challenge that more often than not resulted in a miss or a foul, and then little diagonal loopers that created space by exploiting his opponents' inertia. Riquelme invited close contact, for every defender who approached him was one fewer man hanging all over Crespo.

The gift of a great midfielder is vision, combined with a sense of placement. The aim is to catch your forwards at full speed by putting the ball not where they are but where they will be. The only defense against this kind of attack is speed

---

*Sanchez was vicious in his criticism of Mexico's coach Ricardo La Volpe prior to and during the 2006 Cup. Sanchez made no bones about wanting the job himself, and took over the stewardship of the Mexican national team post-Cup.

and experience. Marquez, the goal-scorer, was the spine of the Mexican back line, and it was his job to make sure the line pulled up *before* Riquelme's through ball, in order to catch Crespo out. This is easier said than done, and defenders must learn to watch their opponents' hips in order to judge the time and angle of their release. (If you only follow the feet and the ball, you can be fooled in the same way a good basketball point guard tricks you with the no-look pass. The angle of the hips, however, never lies, for reasons that have everything to do with gravity and balance.) The offside trap didn't work every time, and Crespo was gifted with one glorious chance midway through the first half that Marquez fortunately squelched.

Mexico, however, was not content to just absorb, and Borgetti, who was determined to make amends, proved himself to be a handful, forcing keeper Roberto Abbondanzieri to make a magnificent individual save and contributing to the run of pressure on the Argentina net that led to one of the most hotly debated decisions of the tournament.

Just as the half was coming to a close, Abbondanzieri rolled the ball out of his area to Gabriel Heinze, a bulky, clever back who is one of the most damaging weapons in Manchester United's arsenal. But Heinze uncharacteristically blanked and didn't settle the ball, creating an opening for Mexico's Francisco "Kikin" Fonseca, who leaped at the ball, won it, and raced netward. Heinze chopped him down to prevent the goal. The controversy arose from what happened next: Heinze had committed a professional foul* and he was also the last

---

*A "professional foul" is a foul that is committed explicitly for the purpose of breaking up play. In other words, Heinze's tackle wasn't malicious, just business. But because such fouls are intentional and premeditated, they are also seen as cynical, and therefore, while the players understand them to be

defender, a combination of circumstances that should have led ref Massimo Busacca to eject him. Instead, Heinze got only a yellow card, Mexico got only a free-kick (which Marquez plowed right into the wall), and Mexico's coach, the Argentine-born Ricardo La Volpe, already incandescent with rage on the sideline, erupted at the ref, unleashing a spectacular torrent of abuse that could be heard in the stands.

The second half could not maintain the pace, and the game settled into a contest steered largely by the one-touch, crisp passing game that is Argentina's hallmark. Yet, despite the late introduction of the teen phenom Lionel Messi (for Javier Saviola) and striker Carlos Tévez (for Crespo), Mexico's defense did not bend. In fact, Mexico held Argentina all game long, forcing the first extra-time game of the second round. Extra time in soccer is not sudden-death: If a game goes into added time, two fifteen-minute "halves" are played out and if the game is still all tied, penalty kicks are taken to decide the winner of a game that ends, officially, as a draw.*

The Argentines took only eight extra-time minutes to win the game, however, and they did so in spectacular fashion. In one of the great individual efforts of the Cup, Maxi Rodriguez collected a cross-field pass from Juan Sorín with his chest, popping it onto his left foot for an incredible volley to the far top corner that eluded Sánchez's leap. It was an artful, and surely instinctive, move and a play of such grace and power that even the Mexican fans had to applaud the effort. Argentina was through to the second round, and Mexico was

---

a part of the game, they enrage fans, coaches, and administrators. A professional foul is an ejectable offense, particularly if it denies a goal-scoring chance.

*Remember this. This is very important in the next chapter.

going home. Despite their disappointment, few of Mexico's fans were truly downcast: Their team had held the great Argentina, and that in itself was a triumph.

Back at my apartment that evening, I heard a Bavarian horn band gamely bloop and honk through what sounded like the same five oompah standards for the "refined" fans eating on a back patio. Out front, however, was the sound of the lumpen, a victorious concerto of car horns and flapping flags, punctuated by the whoops of Argentine and even Mexican fans. Those awful Mohawks mingled with western hats and foam horns in the beer gardens, and I wished I had my own headgear—the giant yellow earmuffs airport ground crews wear.

Unfortunately, fans looking for quality football had to be content with the game in Leipzig. After that spectacular night, the knockout round became very dull, very quickly, and the next day reminded people of just how bad soccer and sports can get.

In 1954 Hungary beat Brazil in one of the most violent international football games ever played. Called the "Battle of Berne," the match saw English referee Arthur Ellis powerless to "prevent some of the ugliest scenes witnessed on a football field," as a correspondent of the time phrased it. Following an injury to a Hungarian player, both teams started brutally fouling each other, and the mayhem only got worse after Hungary converted a disputed penalty kick. Finally, a fight broke out— one that would continue as the players left the field. Ellis was escorted off the pitch by an armed guard.

The night game on June 25, 2006, between Holland and Portugal, might well go down as the modern equivalent. In the "Battle of Nuremburg," Portugal won 1–0, but in reality everyone lost. In an uncharacteristic and still incomprehensible performance, Holland—a team that prides itself on silky movement—somehow allowed itself to be dragged into a dull slog. Only Maniche, the goal scorer, and Arjen Robben and Robin van Persie were at all impressive. Referee Valentin Ivanov let the game spiral out of control early on, and it quickly degenerated into an hour and a half of elbows, studs-up tackles, and a mean-spiritedness rarely seen in the Cup. Portugal's Luís Figo headbutted Mark Van Bommel (not very hard), and the sublime Cristiano Ronaldo, criticized so often for flopping, was this time forced to come off after only a half-hour's work with a very real thigh injury.

Incredibly, sixteen yellow cards were issued and four players—two from each side—were ejected, setting a new record for the Cup. The weird thing about all this was that the Russian ref was actually following the letter of the law, and yet he was lambasted inside and outside the stadium. Ivanov's failure was not in giving out the cards but in giving out so many that he destroyed the flow of the game.* He would not

*This right here encapsulates a nuance of the sport that drives many American sports fans crazy. It is difficult for many U.S. sports fans (whom I find to be an uncommonly statistic-obsessed and rule-stickling bunch compared to the rest of the planet) to accept that sometimes the need to keep things moving along stops refs from calling a foul in soccer. There is a peculiar, almost Puritan, obsession with the letter of the rule in American sports, where the most minor and obscure infractions are parsed with a seriousness and depth other cultures extend only to religious or political discussions. Nowhere else in the world can you tune in on Sunday and listen to four men rigorously dissect, in five-minute intervals while a guy in black and white has his head up a tent, whether Player A was making "a football motion" or was "down by contact," when in reality the topic under discussion can be summed up simply by saying: "Hey, Player A got creamed, huh?" Were only this energy

officiate again after this performance, his international career in tatters after just ninety minutes.

That evening, a heavy rain postgame in Nuremberg defused any potential problems; despite the fans' understandable foul mood, the mayhem was confined to the field.

The day game, between England and Ecuador in Stuttgart, was less violent but equally disappointing. Once again, the Englishmen slogged through a questionable afternoon, with David Beckham forced to rescue the side with a well-taken free kick an hour in. That made him the first English player to have scored in three World Cups, but it was a miserable day out in the heat for the Lions; Beckham vomited on the pitch from dehydration, Wayne Rooney was left adrift by an increasingly feckless English midfielder, and several howlers at the back would have allowed the Ecuadoreans enough daylight to score had they taken their chances. Despite the fact that England was into the quarterfinals, the British media went into meltdown over the performance.

The Italy vs. Australia tie the next day in Kaiserslautern was hotly anticipated, as the Aussies had shown they could play with—if not topple—some of the world's best sides. The Italian fans outnumbered the Aussies in the stands, but the Australians were determined to outshout them, and they did.

Unfortunately, this would be another game decided in large part by refereeing. First, Italian Marco Materazzi was

---

devoted to education and the comfort of the poor. The point is that soccer, because it is a continuous game, makes an implicit bargain with its audience that comes down to this: Not everything is fair, but neither is life, and the game is beautiful, so enjoy it. If you complain about this, as many American soccer geniuses are wont to do, you're considered a whiner. No one likes a whiner.

ejected just after the start of the second half for a comparably innocuous foul on Marco Bresciano. Australia was unable to take advantage of this and, to be honest, never appeared to give much of a threat to the Italians. But the real scandal came in the final minute of the game, when Fabio Grosso charged down the near flank, sauntered into the box, and fell over Lucas Neill, who was already on the ground. Ref Luis Medina Cantalejo immediately pointed the spot, with both players and fans reacting with disbelief. Francesco Totti sunk the penalty kick, time expired, and the Aussies were sent packing.

Most of the planet saw this for what it was: a blatant screwing. It was yet another example of an established team getting the benefit of the doubt at the expense of an upstart, and it cast a pall over the Italian team's progress. Interestingly, FIFA did not discipline Cantalejo; the Spaniard went on to ref in the quarterfinals.

The fact that two games in a two-day period were so affected by the officials drew attention to what has become an emerging problem: how FIFA chooses referees in the first place. The World Cup is unique in that two teams meeting there are highly likely to be overseen by an official from a wholly different continent, with unique nuances that are utterly unfamiliar to the players. FIFA chooses referees for games in a deliberately nonpartisan fashion—the old joke goes that the perfect ref for a Germany vs. Russia game is a Pole, because he hates both sides. It's much harder to pick a man in the middle when a team from Europe plays a team from Africa, and the official chosen may well come from the United States or Asia, where he will have gained his experience in leagues that have little in common with those the players are used to. For example, more cards are issued in

South America than in Europe, as a general rule of thumb. This isn't wrong, just a difference in interpretation, but it can engender frustration, ruin the flow of the match, and distract from the whole point of the exercise. And the officiating issue was exacerbated this Cup by the forced retirement (for age; FIFA's age limit is forty-five) of the one referee in the game unanimously considered both impartial and brilliant: Italian Pierluigi Collina. His retirement left a vacuum at the top of the officiating chain, and not one of the referees of the 2006 Cup distinguished himself enough to fill it.

At least the Italy vs. Australia game got the juices going in a good snit of rightful indignation. The late game between Switzerland and Ukraine on June 26 managed to chill all that off. Mind you, I've had the pleasure of seeing some really awful games: There was a match between Cuba and South Korea where one of the South Korean forwards' shots on net was so badly struck it ricocheted off the corner flag; there was one night in Cowdenbeath, Scotland, where, in an absolute downpour, twenty-two men demonstrated why they would never be mistaken for athletes by anyone save the blind; and more than one game played by the American national team before 1990 was so appalling it was hard to stay awake.

Still, in those cases, there was always a bit of humor to be had, gallows or otherwise. At that Cuba game, I said to myself, "Well, it *is* Cuba, after all," and that made things a little better. China in the late 1990s was comedy gold. They had a team comprised of handsome men who really looked like soccer players. Both the team and their accompanying media bore a confident air that said the Chinese team was going to *win* this game of soccer. And yet, whenever the whistle blew, the players immediately looked like a group of men who had never, ever seen a game of soccer in their lives.*

The game between Switzerland and Ukraine, however, had no redeeming touches. For the first time in my life, had I not been paid to watch, I would have walked away at the half. The problem was stress: Both teams were under so much pressure they were unwilling to take any chances. The ball rarely left the midfield, and camped in front of their own goals the teams looked like armies in trenches, each waiting for the other side to wander into their guns.

One hundred and twenty minutes passed with only three legitimate goal chances. Andriy Shevchenko, the Ukrainian forward who has subsequently struggled at Chelsea, was contained well, with his closest attempt, a header, rattling off the crossbar. His Swiss counterpart, Alexander Frei, also had but one chance, and it, too, clattered across the bar. The match ended deadlocked at 0–0, and penalty kicks were taken. Switzerland missed each attempt, while Ukraine made three straight to progress. The Swiss team thus set two ignominious records: It became the first to be ejected from the World Cup without conceding a goal, and the first to fail to score a single penalty kick in the Cup finals.

On June 27 the last two matches started off simply enough in Dortmund when a seemingly disinterested Brazil

---

*Two things: 1) If you can, go see a China match and spend the day before with their media. This is an ebullient, friendly group supremely convinced of China's acumen right up until about one minute *after* kickoff. At that moment, do yourself a favor and look around. You'll note that all of them look as though they've just been struck with a crippling bowel disorder. 2) I saw one match in which China was so bad I almost convinced myself the wrong team had boarded the plane and this was, in fact, their cricket side. I asked a colleague from Beijing, "Is this *really* the soccer team?" "Oh, yes."

made short work of a Ghana side that looked utterly out-classed from the whistle. In just five minutes Ronaldo scored, thereby collecting his fifteenth goal in his combined Cup finals appearances and passing the Cup scoring record set by West Germany's Gerd Müller. Ghana never looked capable of mounting a serious attack, and when Asamoah Gyan was sent off (for diving, of all things), the Africans' already fragile defense crumbled completely.

Hannover was the venue for the final game, France vs. Spain, the only match of the second round that could be considered a true clash of rivals. I took comfort here in the small signs reminding me that this was, indeed, a world tournament. Flags for Scotland had been seen at every game played so far, and at the AWD Arena a spirited cheering section was in evidence for Mexico.

A man wearing a Chicken Little outfit roamed the grounds, occasionally crowing into a plastic horn. His outfit, a cheerful reference to France's famed *coq sportif,* stood out in a sea of blue jerseys. Across the pitch, signs hanging from the rafters read: THANK YOU GOD FOR SPAIN, joined by a few that, more succinctly, thanked God for Spain's great young midfielder Cesc Fàbregas. Just two summers before he had played in the FIFA U-17 World Cup, where he upstaged Freddy Adu, to the surprise of many American soccer boosters.

This was the best game of the tournament so far, a contest between the old, wily master Zidane and the young maestro Fàbregas that was contentious and absorbing from the kickoff. The teams played distinctive and contrasting styles that were somewhat out of character to boot: France, the smooth-passing, buildup-oriented side, played an immediate game on the night, with Zidane and Patrick Vieira aiming to send Henry through clean for a look at goal. And Franck Ribéry, the scar-faced winger* who emerged in the spring as one of the team's best weapons, was a handful for center-back Carlos Puyol with his darting moves from flank to goal. The Spaniards, on the other hand, were allowing their nineteen-year-old Arsenal midfielder to orchestrate the team in the manner taught by his club coach, Arsène Wenger—smooth, one-touch passing and patience—which Fàbregas had ironically learned at the feet of Vieira.

David Villa put Spain on top early when the aging, hard-nosed French defender Lilian Thuram tomahawked Pablo Ibáñez in the box. But despite chance after chance, Spain would not find the net again. Ribéry equalized off a masterly pass from Vieira just before the half, and France consumed the Spaniards with a seven-minute flurry at the end of the match that produced two goals: the winner, a header from Vieira, and a stoppage-time capper from Zidane, on an errant ball he collected from heir apparent Fàbregas.

For Spain, this was another brutal loss and a reminder to its long-suffering fans of how often this team collapses in must-win games. For France, it was the rebirth of the golden generation in a short forty-five minutes. For soccer fans, it was a symphony.

These eight games presented every note the sport of soccer can hit. The Aussies were furious, seething at the outsize influence the referee can have, murderous at the fakery of Grosso, and yet oddly content. Contrast that with the English, who were busy piling wood around the feet of Sven-Göran Eriksson and

---

*He was badly injured in an auto accident as a child.

their captain, Beckham, despite their being in the quarterfinals. The French were ecstatic at recovering a greatness even their most devout fans had thought lost.

How about the Swiss and the Ukrainians, who demonstrated what a dead-ass game soccer can be at its defensive, timid worst? Or the thuggish Portuguese, who some would argue derailed a younger, less-experienced Dutch side with a cynical game plan aided and abetted by a referee who followed the letter of the law while utterly missing the intent? Could anything be more indicative of the power of this sport than how four games had turned the German nation from reluctant patriots to flag-waving maniacs? And how about the Mexicans, who came, struggled, lost to a world power, and yet went home satisfied? Like the Aussies, they were perfectly happy with losing valiantly.

Does this defy logic? Perhaps, but only if you look at soccer with numbers, by reducing a game and a sport to neat little box scores. It's a weakness of our entertainment culture that there is very little empathy and compassion for loss. Americans prefer to extol great individual performances— say, the swoops of Michael Jordan or the shotgun arm of Satchel Paige—and brush away failure with laughter; think of the oft-mocked Cubs and Browns. This is an attitude hostile to the very nature of soccer. This sport resists easy consumption and disposal; the poor games are often as important as the exciting ones, and the emotional, personal, and patriotic levels on which the sport must be understood bring up scary feelings that often go against what Americans think of as "fun"—one reason, perhaps, soccer has never succeeded on American shores. The rest of the world remembers great soccer *losses,* and broods upon them. Soccer punctures any sense of invincibility a culture has with alarming frequency, and that cuts against the grain of a nation that still has trouble accepting it lost the Vietnam War. The fact is, soccer—with its maniacal crowds, mad tension, and the stifling importance of a single, two-hour stretch of time—is often *not* fun.

So why the heck do people love this sport? Because soccer, as has famously been said, is not religion—it is something far, far more important.

By June 28, the World Cup had ended for most of the competitors. The first round of play was over, and the eight teams left were all from Europe or South America. The Cup had returned to the provincial old guard.

Despite that, the Cup remained a magnet for the entire world. FIFA announced on this day that it estimated thirty billion would watch the 2006 tournament, making it, by far, the most-seen sporting event ever.[*]

But after nineteen straight days of games, the hardest part of the Cup had ended for the people who work behind the scenes. With the upstarts from Asia, the Americas, and Africa sent packing, many accompanying fans, journalists, and officials had left Germany for home. Though the quarterfinals were around the corner, the host cities slowed down with a palpable sense of relief. On June 29 a steady rain fell as Munich just plain took the day off. The beer garden stalls were half open—if at all—and the streets were quiet, as though

---

[*]It would later transpire that FIFA's estimate was not only wildly off-base, but rooted in fiction as well. While the Cup is still by far the best-watched event, for years FIFA has "guessed" or, less charitably, lied about how many people actually watch it. Apparently *three billion* isn't as impressive a figure.

everyone in town was sleeping off the last three weeks in preparation for the weekend.

I had contradictory feelings. The curious thing about covering the Cup, as opposed to seeing it for fun, is that the event moves at such a breakneck pace that by the time you acclimate to it, the thing's almost over. I found myself, perhaps masochistically, wishing for more games left, more fans around, and more soccer to see. It was as though I'd gotten my second wind just as the finish line was crossed.

The truth was I didn't know what to do with myself. "Take a break," my bosses said. I wanted to, but my idea of a nice day off includes watching a soccer game, and this was one of the few days of the year there wasn't one to be had, anywhere in the world. Li, on the other hand, was ecstatic. No guests, no meals to cook or clothes to wash, a husband whose skin seemed a shade less sallow—in the dizzy, artificial world of the Cup, this was like hitting the lottery.

We had an entire café to ourselves for lunch, where we ordered dessert twice. At the Munichstadt Museum, which hosted a major exhibition on the art of soccer, we were the only company for a pair of bored guards who kept whacking a soccer ball into a stairwell. The exhibit was an uneven display, ranging from the pure kitsch of altars dedicated to Argentina's Diego Maradona to the truly inspired: African fertility dolls made to resemble well-known footballers. Curiously, one of these dolls was of Fabian Barthez, who is France's bald, volatile, and erratic goalkeeper, and apparently possessed of libidinal powers hidden from the public at large.

We did what all fans at the Cup were supposed to do: shop. Poking around the shops and alleys that lined the streets of Munich, we rejected an Astroturf covered skirt (too itchy;

prone to falling apart during washing) but snapped up scarves and a handbag cleverly designed to look like a football pitch. We chatted with some American colleagues from ESPN and XM radio, and spent the late afternoon sitting at the lone beer garden open—Mike's small stand that served sausages and dunkel. As we watched, old-timers laughed a group of young, angry neo-Nazi types out of the establishment. The skinheads grumbled, but left. We recognized one of them as the butcher from next door, a young, sullen-looking man who spent most of his days grinding up meat. Even the prostitutes, a friendly bunch, were yawning.

That night, for the first time since the Cup had started, my sleep was uninterrupted by car horns or brass bands or loud young men and women.

The month of June ended with two quarterfinal matches. The German nation, which prides itself on a highly regulated form of capitalism, had spent much of the day trying to cram eight hours into six, leaving just enough time to get to a TV set or out to the Brandenburg Gate to watch one of the massive screens set up for the big game.

This was not a festive day. Germany was playing Argentina, and the country was literally holding its breath. Back when the country was partitioned, West Germany met Argentina twice in the finals. In 1986 Diego Maradona took Argentina past the Germans to the title in Mexico. In Rome, four years later, the tables were turned. That there was some history between the two is a colossal understatement.

One of the most gripping things about a World Cup is that time seems to stop during a big game. When a Super Bowl is on people still go about their business (despite what the overheated announcers might have you think), and during a baseball World Series there are still wide stretches of the country for whom the games mean little. Not so when the host country is playing in a World Cup. During the Germany vs. Argentina game, there was no action on the street at all, so had you been inclined to stage a heist, you could have made a clean getaway between the evening hours of five and seven P.M. Instead of the usual rowdiness, grim silence prevailed during much of the match. The fans were filled with a sense that what was happening in Berlin could be life changing.

Even as deep in Bavaria as I was on June 30,* I felt the Olympic Stadium groan when Roberto Ayala scored after the break to put the South Americans up 1–0. It was hard not to—the entire nation was echoing and amplifying every thought and sound with terrifying precision. When Klose tied up the game with ten minutes left, it was as though every German in the land exhaled for the first time in two hours.

The game went to overtime and then to the cruelest tiebreaker in all sport, the penalty kick. German keeper Jens Lehmann saved two critical penalties to seal his reputation for coolness under pressure, while Argentine backup keeper Leonardo Franco (who had somewhat mysteriously replaced Roberto Abbondanzieri, whose injury did not seem life threatening) could do nothing. The Germans advanced to face Italy. The fans clambered out onto the streets and into their cars, honking horns and waving flags, making a clatter so fulsome it obscured Italy's massacre of an out-of-its-depth Ukrainian side in the late game. But there was an edge to the celebration this night. With the realization that Germany had only to win

---

*I had to remain close to Munich for the semifinal game.

two games to take the trophy, the team—and the country—suddenly had little time for frivolity.

I watched England evaporate against Portugal the next day. Wayne Rooney was sent off in the sixty-second minute—for a foolish attempt to stamp on Ricardo Carvalho's groin—but more damaging was the fact that, when the game ended in a scoreless deadlock, England could find no one competent to take a penalty kick. Ricardo saved Frank Lampard's attempt as well as Steven Gerrard's salvo, then iced it by saving Jamie Carragher's. Eriksson's tenure as England's coach was over.

England's media comforted the nation by whipping up dissent between Rooney and his Manchester United team-mate Cristiano Ronaldo, who had confronted the volatile forward and received a shove for his troubles. Ronaldo was caught on camera winking at his bench as Rooney was sent off, prompting a flurry of questions about sportsmanship and, in a typical display of poor taste, the suggestion that Rooney should have at him* on the Manchester United training grounds. England's players were heartbroken, but the WAGs were in a state of unconcealed glee—they tore out of Baden-Baden while the whistle was still sounding, planning never to return to German soil.

But the real action was yet to come. In 1998, when France hosted the World Cup and *les bleus* faced off against Brazil in the final at the Stade de France, Zidane made his name by running past the fleet-footed men from the favelas, leading France to a 3–0 win and its first World Cup. Now thirty-four,

*Alan Shearer, the former captain of England, was but one of many to advance this argument.

Zidane entered this Cup old in soccer terms and suffering from the toll the sport takes on its players.

This night, however, the old Zidane was on the field, with his skillful passes and insouciant smile. He served in the free kick that produced the greatest goal of the entire tournament, a stunning flick to his old partner Henry. With that, Brazil, world champion just ninety minutes before, was dethroned as king.

A stadium clothed head to toe in yellow sat silent, yellow and green paint dripping off tearful faces to form pools on the concrete. When the whistle blew, the Brazil team looked up at its fans, unmoving and just as stunned. Brazil hadn't been knocked out of a World Cup this early since 1990. Nike-cultured superstars like Ronaldo, Ronaldinho, and Roberto Carlos—household names even in countries that don't care much for the sport—were headed home to Rio in their golden boots instead of catching the train to Berlin. France, in a dazzling and wholly unexpected display, ran 'em right off the field.

Since pizza is the most popular food in America, I thought it fitting to spend my final day in Munich inside an Italian café (the perhaps obviously named Casa del Pizza on Rumford-strasse in Munich) to watch the semifinal between Germany and Italy.

On paper, this was a meeting of the superpowers—the Germans and Italians have both dominated the World Cup—but head to head, the Italians almost always beat their neighbors.

So, in a cramped bar—replete with ceramic taps and a fan that dated from the 1950s—I watched a group of young

Italian men (who made an excellent pizza) explode with the joy unique to the World Cup. They ran into the street. They popped bottles of Proseco. They hugged and kissed all comers. The Germans...well, that was another story. When Fabio Grosso scored, people left without paying. The cook was spit on outside. Drivers honked and tried to run over the waiter's kid, who was playing in the street.

The next day, all the stores that had embraced the World Cup stripped their windows and sales floors of tchotchkes. You could pick up a World Cup pepper mill at half off on July 5 if you liked. Looking for the fun summer clothes with a soccer theme, you found naked mannequins instead. Many chalkboards that had promised WM 2006 LIVE now advertised beer specials. A few cars zipped around with German flags, but many windows that had groaned under red, yellow, and black bunting were now bare. In just twelve short hours, the World Cup had ended here for the Germans, despite the fact that the other semi, the final, and the third-place match (featuring Germany!) were yet to come. It seemed the country was determined to forget the Cup as quickly as possible.

Germans like to talk about the country being an "event-based" culture now, a turn of phrase often applied to the United States and its love of big-ticket shows like the Olympics or Lollapalooza. The truth, though, is that the love of the sport and the meaning of the World Cup here ran far deeper than this cozy brush-off.

So, on July 5, Germany was a country in mourning. The signs came down, and the face paint was wiped off. But people still winced when cars beeping their horns drove by sporting big Italian flags.

THE CITY OF GHOSTS

"Welcome to the World Cup in Germany," said the train's conductor as my wife and I arrived, bleary-eyed, in Berlin. "You know, the one we lost."

I had pulled an all-nighter in Munich, covering France's 1–0 win over Portugal,* getting back to the flat in Munich around two A.M., and then heading out to catch the earliest train to Berlin. I had another two days off and figured I might as well spend them in the capital, soaking up its famous atmosphere.

What to make of this city? Most other German cities seemed fairly straightforward, if not exactly "easy" to figure out. Munich was plain and open; Kaiserslautern was suffocating; and Nuremberg was creepy. But Berlin was unlike any of them, and unlike the rest of Germany to boot. It was raw, and weird, and thanks to a combination of heat, fatigue, and bizarre German medications, it didn't seem entirely real to me from the start. By the end of my stay I was seriously wondering whether someone had slipped me a half-dozen hits of acid somewhere along the line.

---

*A game so unremarkable I am sparing you a description of it.

We stayed in a decaying riverside "artist's hotel" on Fried-richstrasse, a place with an ice cream parlor on the bottom floor, a roped-off lower level, rooms with pools in them, and a winding staircase—at the top of which, on the day I moved in, a gay porn film was being shot. It was pretty tough to miss. To get to my room, I had to step over the cables for the lights, avoid a woman wearing a towel, and pass an open room where two dark-skinned men were frantically coupling. The men were visibly straining for erotic effect but the film crew looked bored. The director gave orders in a calm, unaffected voice while the woman leaned against the wall, carelessly flicking ashes on the carpet and staring into space. I almost fell over the cable running down the stairs. The cameraman, a porcine man sweating badly through a too-short shirt, asked me to hand him a soda from the cooler and offered me one with a gesture. I put down my luggage, the crew took five, and I drank a German Coke knockoff with them while craft services handed out fresh condoms and lube. The only con-versation during this frankly bizarre experience was when the director leaned in close to me, jabbed his thumb back toward the working guys, and said, "For Algeria."

When I reached the room, the first thing Li said to me was, "So, didja see the fuck flick in the pool room? I wouldn't want to swim in that water."

We changed and went back out, and saw that the film crew was packed and gone: They had rented the suite by the hour.

Berlin would be like this during our stay—half chilling and half slapstick. Ruined buildings sat side by side with lav-ish malls; chunks of the Berlin Wall lay next to new apart-ments; and the city was covered in explosive and at times exuberant graffiti, in sharp contrast to the slick billboards hawking expensive products. During the tournament, the city was also unbelievably hot. The roads shimmered and the Spree River, which had triggered thoughts of a cooling boat trip, acted as a giant reflector, scorching all who would dare venture onto it. Both the river and our neighborhood carried historic baggage. From our window, we could look across the water to the so-called Palace of Tears, a partition-era addition to the Friedrichstrasse S-Bahn where Easterners said good-bye to their Western friends and families. Today it is a trans-vestite bar.

Berlin's history is convoluted. Once a hamlet built on marshes at the banks of the Spree, Germany's most important city (and on-and-off capital) since the 1400s is one of the most battle-torn in Europe, having been sacked a half-dozen times as a military prize since the Thirty Years' War, a conflict that cost the city half its population. Berlin was the seat of the Prussian Empire until Napoléon took it. (He generously gave the city self-rule.) World War I devastated it. The Weimar Re-public and its culture, which sprang up from the ashes of that fierce conflict, were profoundly influenced by streets full of crippled, shell-shocked soldiers. In the World War II era, the city was the capital of the Reich until 1945, when the Red Army arrived. The city was first divided in 1948,* and the fa-mous Berlin Wall erected in 1961. That concrete barrier fell in 1989, and Germany is still dealing with the painful process of

---

*On June 24, 1948, the Berlin Blockade began when the Soviet Union closed road and rail access to all of the Western sectors following a dispute over reparations and administration. The Blockade was lifted on May 11, 1949, after the success of the Berlin Airlift operation carried out by Allied forces.

reunification. Yet despite being ground zero in three world-wide conflicts in the past century alone, Berlin retains an uncommon breeziness and sophistication.

It was fitting I'd run headfirst into a porno in Berlin: The city's reputation for licentiousness dates back to the 1920s, when poverty and dislocation created one of the first destinations for what is today called "sex tourism." Back then, folks like writers W. H. Auden and Christopher Isherwood traveled to a city that tolerated homosexuality, prostitution, and pederasty and offered just about anything for a price.

All of this took place in a highly charged postwar atmosphere* where shame over Germany's failure in the Great War, economic hardship, and a dazzling array of political opportunists and idealists formed a fast and explosive scene. Cabarets and cafés offered everything from highfalutin theater to hookers and opiates; real literary and artistic genius mingled with crackpot theorists; and the still-new Brownshirts brawled with Communists in the streets. The truth is, Berlin—which once was two distinct cities (Cologne and Berlin)—was a divided city long before the Wall.

Berlin remains an artist's and expat's mecca: Living is comparatively cheap, and the city has a well-earned reputation for producing excellent modern electronic music as well as nurturing local DJs. (Until this past year, Berlin also hosted two competing major electronic music festivals, the well-known Love Parade and the lesser-known Fuckparade.†) In

---

*See chapter 3 for more.

†This is a shortened version of the "real" name, which is Fuck the Love-parade. The festival is run by a group upset with the perceived commercialism of the Love Parade. The Love Parade was held, apparently for the final time, on July 15, 2006.

terms of high art, however, today's Berlin has yet to rival the Weimar Republic, when George Grosz, Otto Dix, Fritz Lang, Bertolt Brecht, Max Beckmann, and others turned the horror of war and depression into some of the most visceral works of art, music, and film ever produced. Their heir might be the painter Anselm Kiefer; fittingly Berlin plans to open a museum dedicated to him.

The Alexanderplatz, which I had desperately wanted to visit—both because of the famous Fassbinder film and because of the role the square played in Weimar culture in the 1920s—was a grave disappointment. The *platz* is now a seedy, asphalt-covered plaza, surrounded by what looked like long-abandoned roadwork and filled with aimless youths drinking cheap beer. The Fernsehturm, the giant TV tower that overlooks the area, was painted in T-Mobile's magenta to resemble a soccer ball, but it still looked ominous, like a guard tower overseeing the former GDR. In fact, the tower was built by the East German government in 1969, and was used, in part, to beam out propaganda and jam any Western signals coming in.*

Once the colorful center of Berlin nightlife, the whole area looked depressed—a lot of small shops were shuttered, and the only real moments of joy came around the Neptunbrunnen, a giant fountain where kids were splashing and playing. Nearby, oversize statues of Karl Marx and Friedrich Engels patiently waited for attention. None was forthcoming.

Disappointed in the Alexanderplatz, we went to see the remains of the Berlin Wall and the new museum, where we ran into a friend and colleague of mine who was out for a jog.

---

*This was not, however, the source of the "Russian Woodpecker," an infamous signal that played havoc with shortwave radios across the world.

He stepped gamely in place, damp and sweating, as we looked over what once had been deadly to cross. Today a junk market, a cemetery, and an open field occupy the site.

Near Checkpoint Charlie, we visited a handful of the bars where Communism was once debated over thin glasses of Kölsch and syrupy Weisse. Sitting in the shadows of buildings that once housed the aristocracy, I could see how the idea of a workers' paradise became so seductive.

On the night of the third-place match, July 8, we took a walk along the Unter der Linden, the tree-lined double-wide boulevard that ends at the Brandenburg Gate. The gate was the epicenter of World Cup football in Berlin: where the massive viewing parties were held, where TV crews congregated, and where you went to celebrate.

A giant, blue neon-illuminated soccer ball was parked just before the gate with its photogenic quadriga, a statue of a horse-drawn chariot. The blue orb was a combination World Cup shop and ready-made TV backdrop, and the little traffic turnaround was crowded with bulky cables, cameras, and fans. On the other side of the gate, Berlin's police corralled most of the fans into a massive, semi-roped-off area.

That night in faraway Stuttgart, Germany was busy seeing off Portugal in a game neither team really wanted to play. Bastian Schweinsteiger scored twice in the second half for the Germans while Petit tucked in an own goal to give the hosts an unassailable lead. Nuno Gomes got some consolation late in the game for the Portuguese, but the match ended 3–1. It was a fitting finale for the German team, which had been brutally disappointed against Italy. It had lost the semifinal game in added time, thanks to the skill of the oft-maligned Andrea Pirlo, who cleanly beat Jens Lehmann with a pass to Fabio

Grosso in literally the final minute. Grosso, the villain against Australia, reduced the German fans and team to tears. The team was so stunned that, as it pushed forward in desperation, Alessandro Del Piero found an opening to chip another one in before the whistle blew.

After the Portugal game, we walked along the Spree River among the thousands of fans—a shocking number of whom seemed to be on a corporate junket—and sensed a lot of passion but no substance. Fans spilled out of bars, cheerfully singing. Down the road, Adidas had set up its own fan festival and viewing area, and kids and adults were pouring out into the streets. This was a celebration, sure . . . but for what? For soccer—or just for the sake of a party, for music, booze, and money? On the steps of the Reichstag, hundreds of people sat quietly enjoying the evening; they paid little attention to the big screens, the spotlights, or the music. We walked past a giant aspirin pill on the Reichstagufer, erected as part of the "Land of Ideas" exhibit that elevated a handful of common objects to monumental stature during the Cup. Germany might be the home of Bayer, but given our trouble obtaining pharmaceuticals here, the statue seemed ironic.

The final showcased two of the world's best teams. Italy, three-time Cup winners and practitioners of a defensive style of football both intensely technical and, on occasion, very boring, was to face a French team surprised to be in the championship match.

France's linchpin was Zinedine Zidane, universally considered one of the greatest players ever to grace the game. Like England's Wayne Rooney, Zidane grew up poor, a child of Algerian Kabyle* immigrants in the hardscrabble port town of Marseille in Southern France. Like the Man U star, the Frenchman grew up in a bleak housing project, La Castellane, and, as with Rooney, religion played a role in his upbringing. Zidane is a Muslim, albeit nonpracticing, in an overwhelmingly Christian country struggling with the issue of immigration and the question of "Frenchness."

Those questions came to a head when France hosted the World Cup in 1998. Right-wing politician and gadfly Jean-Marie Le Pen slammed the French squad, as "Black, Blanc, and Beur,"† by saying it did not "represent the true France." Le Pen would repeat his criticisms in 2006, saying France could "not recognize herself" in a lineup that included seventeen black players. In truth, the French national team has long been integrated, having fielded black Frenchmen as far back as 1931 (Raoul Diagne, for example), and boasts a long line of multicultural stars.

Zidane was not a prodigy like Rooney, but he was spotted early and developed in AS Cannes' youth system from the age of fourteen. He had a respectable career at Bordeaux, helping the club win the 1995 Intertoto Cup and leading it to second place in the 1995–96 UEFA Cup. After that, everything changed for Zidane: Juventus, one of the great Italian clubs, signed him for $5 million and he blossomed into the superstar the world knows today.

---

*The Kabyle people are Berbers and speak a distinct language. They make up one of the largest ethnic minority groups in Algeria.
†*Beur* is French slang for people of North African origin. It is not considered offensive. I assume Le Pen chose "Black" instead of "Noir" for alliterative purposes.

Zidane's greatness comes not from his power or speed, but from his ability to see the entire field and anticipate the outcome of a cross or series of passes before they occur. Most times it seems as though Zidane is doing very little. But those innocent movements can suddenly flash into a defense-splitting pass or a ferocious goal. What makes Zidane truly special is not that he can control the pace of a match—there are other holding midfielders in the game—but that his motions and his instincts are artful, serene, and beautiful.

A remarkable film debuted in France prior to the Cup. The film consists of a single camera fixed on Zidane for the duration of one game. You see him walk, look, shuffle back, perhaps run a little. For the majority of the film, he seems to do nothing at all. And then, suddenly, he leaps forward, takes the ball with a single touch, and strokes it ahead into space, just where his forward is about to be. You cannot tell how he got the ball, or how he knew where his teammate would appear. But he did, and then, once again, he is doing nothing. The scene changes your perception of the film, from sleep-inducing to hypnotic. For a split second you realize you're seeing magic.

Zidane does this often enough that he has been named the world's best player a record three times. When profligate Real Madrid wanted to add him to their roster of *galacticos*, it cost the Spaniards €66 million (nearly $131 million) to pry him loose from Turin. And when France won its first-ever World Cup in 1998, everyone knew who was responsible. So effective is Zidane that when the French unexpectedly flopped in the succeeding World Cup, most observers ascribed it to Zidane's poor form. He had tried to return too quickly from injury and was a noticeably different player.

Zidane's gift for timing extended off the field. He had announced his retirement from the sport prior to the tournament, and even after a string of fine performances in the latter stages of the Cup, the calls for him to return sounded hollow. He knew it was time to go, and this final was his last chance to make his mark.

You reach the Olympic Stadium via a short elevated train ride through a forested area and a walk past where the dormitories of the 1936 Games once stood. The press center was parked on one of the fields that surround the stadium, and the first thing reporters saw were the old security towers—tall, thin, vaguely medieval constructions with slit windows and all the charm of a high-rise. Below and in front of them were the 1930s friezes depicting the various Olympic sports in the faux Hellenistic style favored by the Nazis, along with a cluster of titanic nude athletes sculpted by Arno Breker.

Milling around these bizarre artworks was a crowd very different from any other at this World Cup. More than half the tickets for the final went to sponsors and hangers-on, and these well-heeled spectators, there to see and be seen, were chiefly interested in the wine-and-cheese tent. The small groups of French and Italian fans—many of whom were begging for tickets—were overwhelmed by slim young things in suits and slip dresses, blithely sipping beer and chatting about money. The atmosphere of style and cash made the Cup final seem as cold and soulless as the old stadium and, for me, summed up everything that is wrong about the game and the selling of the sport of soccer today.

I walked into the match with a colleague, Amy Lawrence. From the catwalk that took us directly to the press loge, we could see the former Olympic brazier, the viewing area where Hitler and his officials watched Jesse Owens triumph at the Games and where, today, at the Marathon Gate, the singer Shakira would perform an interminable, loopy version of her song "Hips Don't Lie."

I told Amy, who is Jewish, that I thought the whole setting was intensely creepy, and she surprised me by saying she disagreed: "I think it's rather uplifting, actually. We're here, and they're not. We won."

We squeezed into our seats, crammed in almost unbreathably tight. Despite the hokey buildup and the consumerism, here, inside the stadium, there was an electricity. The crowd sensed something big was about to happen and they saw a spectacular, aggressive match, featuring the best of both teams. In the end Italy took home its fourth Cup, a feat excelled only by Brazil's five.

Yet, like so much of this Cup on the field, the final will forever be remembered not for the result, but for ugliness. The game was tainted by referee Horacio Elizondo's failure to correctly award a penalty call when Florent Malouda was felled by Marco Materazzi in the box in the fifty-first minute, but it was Zidane who laid the hammer blow.

"The headbutt" has become an indelible image for the man and for the sport. It shook apart a game that until that point had shown how dominating the thirty-four-year-old midfielder could be, and put a sad coda onto what was one of the greatest careers in the sport. Zidane ended his long and glorious run by being ejected in extra time, arguably costing France the Cup.

At the moment in the stadium, there was chaos—half the crowd had seen the headbutt and the other half had no idea what had happened. We saw it on replay in the press booth, and our hearts sank. The sight of Zidane stopping, turning slowly around, and pacing back to blast Materazzi in the chest was incomprehensible. What had happened? It seemed to come out of nowhere. Elizondo consulted with the linesman while the crowd stewed. What could have been said to cause the great man to lose his cool? And yet, when Elizondo raised his hand with the red card in it and Zidane walked off, his face was curiously blank. He then looked stunned.

People across the globe tried to coax out what Materazzi had said to Zidane, and newspapers hired lip-readers and put the full-gang press on to decode what was suddenly the most important exchange in the sport's history.

Having some experience with lipreading myself,* I huddled with a group of English, Italian, and French reporters to review the tape. We came to a consensus†: Materazzi had called Zidane the "son of a terrorist whore" in Italian, and then told him to "go fuck himself." The French players weren't talking, though one let slip to journalists that the insult was personal

---

*My father's father was almost totally deaf due to a series of strokes and was a lip-reader the entire time I knew him. He taught me this skill when I was young, after I wondered why he couldn't hear me if I wasn't facing him. I started having my own hearing difficulties in the early 1990s—the result of a previous career as a musician and a night in Rochester, New York, where my amplifier served as my monitor, with disastrous results—and I have found myself relying more and more on this skill in everyday life since then.
†Later, the London *Times*'s hired pro also came to this conclusion; the Brazilian press also reported that Materazzi had called Zidane's mother a "prostitute."

in nature* and another, who plays in Italy, confirmed the "terrorist" jibe. (Materazzi responded with this outrageous statement: "I don't even know what a terrorist is."†)

Few remember that France was the better team. And fewer still remember that it was a great match. Italy was put back on its heels early, after Florent Malouda was toppled by Materazzi in the box in just the sixth minute. An insouciant Zidane chipped the ball over keeper Gianluigi Buffon, bouncing it off the crossbar and over the line.

But Italy struck back with a smothering offense that was rewarded in the nineteenth minute when Andrea Pirlo, serving up a razor-wire corner kick, found the head of his defender to allow Materazzi to make amends. Materazzi's header cleanly beat Fabian Barthez, and the momentum shifted gravely.

With Pirlo and Mauro Camoranesi running hard at the shaky Eric Abidal on the flank, increased pressure was put on the steady Lilian Thuram and William Gallas and for a time it looked as though the *azzurri* could turn the game into a rout. Pirlo almost repeated the trick in the thirty-fourth when Luca Toni rocketed a header off the crossbar following a corner.

But the momentum swung back France's way for good after the break, with *les bleus* shifting tactics to envelop wide men Franck Ribéry and Malouda into what had been a two-man attack. With Thierry Henry finally finding his touch the French began disrupting what had been an impressive Italian

---

*This turned out to be true: Materazzi later admitted he had insulted Zidane's sister, then claimed he didn't even know Zidane had one.
†This was in Italian, and is translated.

defense, forcing bad mistakes and compressing the Italians into the back half of the field.

Italian captain Fabio Cannavaro, the man who would later triumphantly hoist the trophy, was the difference. As Genarro Gattuso and Fabio Grosso were made increasingly superfluous by an unrelenting barrage orchestrated by Thuram, sub Alou Diarra, and Zidane, Cannavaro held the line. The closest the French came was in the 100th minute, when Ribery pushed his shot just wide. Zidane followed three minutes later with a blinding header that Buffon palmed over the bar.

Seven minutes after that, Zidane was sent off. Shaking off the legacy of Roberto Baggio's missed penalty kick in 1994, Italy sank five straight kicks to win the Cup, with Grosso sinking the winner. For the first time in four tries the Italians had won a championship in the tiebreaker.

"Zidane being sent off killed us," said coach Raymond Domenech. "We can only be disappointed, not by our run but by the way it ended. Really, from the game we played, we deserved to win."

Domenech stayed away from questions of what could have provoked Zidane, saying only, "There are moments . . . sometimes when you are hit for eighty or ninety minutes. I'm not saying I'm excusing it but I can understand."

In the days that followed, Zidane's mother supposedly told reporters that she wanted the Italian's "balls on a platter."* Zidane apologized for letting down France, but not for

---

*This was reported in the less-than-credible English tabloid the *Daily Mirror*, and purportedly came from "friends." Since his mother was recovering from an illness at the time, it seems unlikely she ever said this.

striking Materazzi: In a closely watched interview televised on Canal+—the only time he discussed the subject—Zidane stated that the insult concerned his mother and sister, and said, "I can't regret my actions because that would mean he had the right to say what he did. I can't, I can't say that. No, he didn't have the right to say what he did."* Materazzi, who did not deny insulting Zidane, did however maintain that he had not insulted Zidane's mother, and the Italian press was quick to note that Materazzi lost his own mother at fifteen.

Footage of the headbutt circled the globe at a startling rate—by the time I was back at my hotel, a video game based on the incident was making the rounds. Zidane's shot to Materazzi's chest also helped propel an emerging form—the viral video—into mass consciousness. An inestimable number of video clips were seen via mobile phone, e-mail, and Web sites, with over sixteen hundred video clips viewed more than four million times on the then nascent YouTube site alone. There was even a subset of imitators and parodies, plus a compilation of Materazzi's own on-field hatchet jobs.

On one side of the car were the French fans. On the other were the Italian fans, ecstatic at having overcome history to win the Cup on penalty kicks. The sides sat uneasily across from each other as the subway pulled out of Zoo station just after the game. No one seemed sure what to make of the match, and those who spoke talked in low, hushed tones about "Zizou."

Trouble flared when an Italian fan bumped into another young woman, who was dressed up like a classic French

*In French; this is translated for your benefit.

mime. The mime's hot drink splashed onto the back of the Italian woman's leg, and she turned around and began yelling, whereupon the Frenchwoman tossed the full cup of tea into her face. A large crowd gathered and police waded in.

A rambunctious group of Italian fans cheerfully taunted their French counterparts with shouts of: *"Chi sono i campioni del mondo? Italia!"** They followed that up with a cheer for Zidane, who was clearly already being remembered as the villain of the night. The French fans took this in good stride, however, joining in cheers for both Italy and France.

We finally left Berlin's main train station at two A.M., stepping around the fans sleeping on the floor as they waited for the next train out. Every car was packed and sold out six times over—anyone who hadn't gotten a ticket was stuck in Berlin. Fans were bedding down for the night under bridges, in the station, anywhere they could find.

One sad young French fan made her way down the platform, heading toward her makeshift bed of luggage and newspaper. She was dressed in horns and a flowing white skirt—Asterix meets Marianne[†]—and her red and white face paint had run down, staining her blue French jersey. She drank her coffee, and she cried.

---

*"Who are the champions of the world? Italy!"
[†]A wildly popular European cartoon hero; the national symbol of France.

10

THE AFTERMATH

After spending six weeks in Germany, I came to a number of conclusions. The first was that I never wanted to have a beer again. The second was that the World Cup is still a special event, but not for soccer. Today's World Cup is special for the nationalism it affords, for its TV ratings, and, most of all, for the money.

One of the books I brought along to read with me on long German train rides was Guy Debord's *Comments on the Society of the Spectacle.** In it, Debord makes the point that spectacles are self-replicating and all consuming. In other words, something like the World Cup, which will be remembered for being a big party, may no longer be remembered as anything *but* a big party. This makes the Fan Fests one of the

---

*I am sure the late (and rather nihilistic) Mr. Debord would feel that no member of the media could ever grasp his arguments—he viewed the press as an integral part of what he believed to be an increasingly "Americanised" [sic] and commercial society. He also probably would have been horrified at the "Americanisation" of the Cup, to say nothing of Paris Saint-Germain's performance in the French league last year. This book was a follow-up to *The Society of the Spectacle,* which was a seminal text in . . . um, well, the 1968 Paris student riots.

biggest—and potentially damaging—legacies of the 2006 World Cup. This may be a generalization, but it seems to me that Germany's staging of the Cup, with the relentless emphasis on consumerism and the "good time," may have forever altered what the World Cup is and what it will be in the future. The World Cup is now first and foremost a spectacle—and as such may ultimately weaken what it was meant to celebrate.

Zidane's exit in the final not only took France's chances with him but emphasized the sad fact that the best soccer in the world is no longer showed at the Cup. Overall, this was an exceptionally poorly played Cup with the best players arriving worn out from their club duties.

Perhaps the dullest, most cynical Cup was Italia 1990. Penalty shoot-outs were needed to decide both semifinals, and every neutral fan on the night of the final was secretly thanking the Mexican referee for awarding the German side the penalty that ended a terrible Argentina vs. West Germany match. But out of that tournament's mess came action: FIFA recognized that bigger, faster defenders and midfielders, far superior scouting and training methods, and much smarter coaching had tilted the balance of the game. So: Game-destroying back passes to goalkeepers, often from the halfway line, could no longer be picked up; professional fouls were punished with automatic red cards; and goalkeepers were sent off for killing attacks by deliberately handling balls outside their areas. These changes were designed to give the attackers a better chance and to open up a game that had become entangled in its own defensive schemes.

As a result, fans saw pretty good—if not exactly ground-breaking—stuff from the 1994, 1998, and 2002 Cups, yet that delicate attack-defense balance remained in jeopardy. Over time, the edge the attackers were supposed to have was slowly eroded by linesmen who too often flagged for offside and by referees who too often favored defenders over the forwards.

Ironically, the Champions League helped solve that problem, as clubs began assembling specialized teams made up of the world's best players. By doing so, they have improved the level of club play to such an extent that it is folly to believe now that even the best national side could succeed in that six-month competition. The downside is that the Champions League elite has also served to dilute national team talent by wearing out the very stars that once made countries special. It was no accident that France and Argentina (to name just two) arrived in South Korea and Japan with tired players who seemed to have little interest in exhausting themselves further after playing a year's worth of "must-win" matches. It is also not a coincidence that many of the predicted stars of Germany 2006 didn't shine, most prominently Brazil's Ronaldinho and France's Thierry Henry. Both, of course, had played in the Champions League final a mere three weeks before the World Cup kicked off. Neither seemed to have his legs in Germany, and nonsoccer fans watching them play for the first time must have wondered what all the fuss was about.

Once, players made their world debuts at the Cup. In 1958 Pelé came onstage at the age of seventeen, lighting up the Swedish World Cup and sparking perhaps the single greatest national team ever, Brazil 1970. We saw new playing styles emerge from 1974 with Holland's "total football" and Franz Beckenbauer's creation of the attacking center back, the *"libero."* Closer to home, American Alexi Lalas would never have played in Italy, and Cobi Jones, Brad Friedel, or Carlos Bocanegra would probably not have had their chances overseas, if not for the 1994 Cup and how it changed the perception of American players worldwide.

Where at the 2006 Cup were all those "unknowns" we should have met from "small" countries like Ivory Coast or South Korea? When Haiti and Zaire arrived in West Germany in 1974 it is safe to say not even the best-informed soccer journalist in Europe could have named their starters or told you much about their players. But in 2006 it turned out that the best player Ivory Coast possessed was a fellow named Didier Drogba, whom we saw every week with Chelsea. And South Korea's midfield dynamo, Park Ji-Sung, just happens to play for Manchester United. Today the idea that a World Cup can introduce new players and showcase new tactics seems quaint. These days there are no dark horses to spring an upset simply because everyone is on the radar—and signed by a top club.

Heading into Germany, the pundits looked at rosters and saw players' names, and were dazzled by their clubs. This was a major miscalculation, as few of us took into account how many teams now play deep into May each season, forcing their top talent to produce fifty-five to sixty times a year. This is something new—even when Pelé's Santos was snapping up every dollar it could by barnstorming around the world, that great man never played sixty high-level matches in a season. There's a reason why the ageless Romário is still scoring goals for Brazil's Vasco da Gama—he isn't facing the top defenders in the world every time he takes the field. And there's a reason why fellow Brazilian Ronaldo's goal production has tumbled: He is.

What FIFA needs to figure out is how to get the level of competition in the World Cup back to where it was two decades ago. That's not going to be easy, because the big clubs—and global satellite television—are increasingly calling the tune. Like the Olympics, which have had to adapt to the age of open, professional sports, the World Cup may well need a complete makeover soon.

The best things about the Cup remain unique, however. An insipid pseudopatriotism, a flat-out lie, surrounds the Olympics and obscures the truth that there really isn't much interest in many of the events that fill the calendars of the winter and summer Games. A World Cup, however, touches the national soul like no other sporting event. I returned to the United States and heard Italian Americans recount where they were on the day of the championship match. One had watched it with his father—the old man danced around the living room like a child. Another had his wedding planned for the day of the final, but rescheduled rather than miss the game. (His wife had been furious... at the thought they might miss the game.) People may not necessarily think of themselves as soccer fans, but they do think of their origins, and the World Cup gives them a potent excuse for celebration. In that sense, the fact that Champions League soccer is better than World Cup soccer probably doesn't matter.

But the World Cup's importance has always been to showcase and extend the reach of the game. For instance, for many fans the Mexican World Cup of 1986 is remembered as the event that transformed soccer from a Euro-Latin American fascination into a global sport. To continue to do that, the Cup must retain the magic that always defined it.

FIFA needs a Ronaldinho to excel at its event, just as Pelé did in 1958.

FIFA needs the world to see a new style at its event, as it did with Holland in 1974.

That was lost in Germany for a myriad of reasons. FIFA now faces a major challenge to keep the World Cup at the center of the world game.

After the tournament:

The incident at the final became an Internet phenomenon, and a song about the headbutt later went to number one on France's pop charts.

Zinedine Zidane revealed nothing more about what had been said to him. He retired and dropped out of view, resurfacing only to play a friendly match for charity. When contacted by the American league MLS, Zidane declined to enter serious negotiations, despite a reported offer of $15 million from the Chicago Fire.

Thierry Henry, in a shock move, was sold by Arsenal to Spanish rival Barcelona in June 2007 for $32 million.

His nemesis, Marco Materazzi, went on to make the most of his newfound celebrity. Once widely considered a hoodlum in Italy—you can easily find online compilations of his more egregious fouls—Materazzi awoke the day after the final to find himself rehabilitated. Shortly after the Cup he published a book entitled *What I Really Said to Zidane*, a collection of 249 pithy quotes that included this gem: "French philosophy has been rubbish since Foucault died."* Proceeds

---

*Ironically, post–World Cup, Foucault's work was given a thorough hatchet job in the *Times Literary Supplement* after a new release of *Madness and Civilization* revealed how tenuous his historical sources were. Just saying.

from the book were donated to charity. Zidane, asked by French TV station Canal+ about the book, indicated he was not amused. Efforts to reconcile the two players have failed as of this writing.

England's David Beckham returned to Spanish club Real Madrid, where after a poor start to the season he was benched by new coach Fabio Capello. Beckham, in the final year of his contract with the club, then made a move that garnered world headlines: He agreed to join the MLS club Los Angeles Galaxy in July 2007 in a contract that could ultimately pay him $250 million. Beckham's arrival was eagerly awaited in the United States.

His teammate Wayne Rooney returned to Manchester United and helped lead that club to a winning season. Manchester United won two out of the four major trophies, including the Premier League.

German coach Juergen Klinsmann resigned and returned to his family in California.

U.S. Soccer did not renew Bruce Arena's contract and, in a reportedly tense three-hour meeting at an airport hotel, relieved him of his duties. Arena subsequently signed a contract worth $1.4 million a year, an enormous sum for the MLS, to coach the New York Red Bulls. U.S. Soccer then went on a very public flirtation with Klinsmann that ended badly when the German, after agreeing on compensation, abruptly stiffed the organization, seriously damaging the credibility of new president Sunil Gulati.

Clint Dempsey played out the rest of the season with New England, leading that team to the MLS Cup final, where it lost on penalty kicks after a scoreless draw. On a $4 million transfer Dempsey subsequently joined Fulham in England, where he began fighting for a place as the club struggled to avoid relegation.

Bob Bradley served as the interim coach after Arena was relieved, and subsequently was named the new head coach. He steered the USA to a successful defense of its CONCACAF Gold Cup title in June 2007 and was preparing to take the USA to Copa America as this book went to press.

The manager of the Berlin World Cup venue, Jürgen Kiessling, walked out of his house the day after the final, put a gun to his head, and shot himself. He left two suicide notes, neither of which has been released.

Dave O'Brien and Marcelo Balboa shrugged off the bad reviews and can be seen every week on ESPN and HDNet in the United States. O'Brien also signed a deal to broadcast for the Boston Red Sox. Due to the tremendous ratings the World Cup received, ESPN, ABC, Fox, and Univision all paid MLS broadcast rights, and the quality of game telecasts has noticeably improved.

The match-fixing scandal in Italy came to a less-than-satisfying close when an appeals panel threw out a series of tough punishments for the clubs involved. After a round of transparent politicking, five clubs were hit with points penalties and Juventus was forced to relinquish its last two titles and was demoted to the Italian second division. Italian clubs were still allowed to compete in European club competitions, and most saw the moves as little more than a slap on the wrist. That viewpoint was borne out by a season that saw Juventus play to packed houses and get promoted to the first division, while the other teams overcame their penalties and avoided the drop. At the close of the investigation, a new series of allegations roiled the country once more.

AC Milan won the 2007 edition of the Champions League, beating Liverpool in the final at Athens, 2–1. Many people felt that AC Milan should not have even been allowed into the tournament in the first place, and UEFA has changed the rules to prevent clubs under suspicion from competing in future editions of the Champions League.

Post–World Cup, violence flared across Europe. In Leipzig, thirty-nine police officers were injured in February 2007 when fans rioted after a game between fifth-division teams. The same month in Italy, Catania had its stadium shuttered, after a policeman was killed following a riot that consumed the Sicilian city before a game against Palermo. In early April Manchester United fans were attacked by "ultra" fans and beaten by policemen in Rome during a Champions League quarter-final tie. Eighteen were hospitalized and UEFA opened an investigation.

The 2006 World Cup was remembered as something of a golden moment for Germany. According to the German government, retail sales during the Cup grew by 1.9 percent; the HDE retail association estimated the event generated €2 billion ($2.7 billion) in extra sales. The German Football Association managed to earn some €21 million, which it promptly spent on fields and clubs. Yet, after the Cup, the same old depressing news began again: The Bundesliga's teams were finding it increasingly hard to compete at the very top, as England and Spain sucked away many of the best players; the town scheduled to host the G-8 summit apparently still had Hitler as an honorary citizen; and, in a training film that fulfilled every stereotype possible, a German army instructor urged his charges to fight by telling them to view their opponents as poor blacks from the Bronx, "who had just said the most awful things about your father."

The United States is still fighting in Iraq and Afghanistan.

Sepp Blatter is still FIFA's president, and both he and Jack Warner ran unopposed for their respective positions in elections in 2007. Warner was reprimanded by FIFA for trying to sell World Cup tickets to Trinidad and Tobago at a personal profit, but received no significant punishment.

I returned home to Chicago, where I suffered a grand mal seizure and subsequently had neurosurgery, delaying the publication of this book.

The World Cup will return in 2008, as qualifying for the 2010 finals in South Africa begins.

ACKNOWLEDGMENTS

There are many people without whom this book could not have been written. Hopefully, this list manages to credit them all.

First and foremost is Li, who saw her first trip to Germany transformed into a whole mess of work combined with panic, chaos, and babysitting for a good dozen people. She didn't expect to become secretary, chef, event and financial planner, and meds wrangler, but she did it with a grace and support that I completely don't deserve. Through thick and thin, she was the voice of reason, and is my biggest fan. So, thank you, Li.

Matt McGowan at Goldin Literary Agency was not only the instigator of this project but has been solidly in my corner, coolly dealing with one thing after another as the schedule went from four months to eleven. The guy has ice in his veins. The same is true for editor Stacia Decker, who showed infinite patience in the face of unforeseen events. Both of them helped me develop the voice you will find in these pages, and I am deeply indebted to them.

It would perhaps be a better story if I were the cliché "writer who overcame a miserable childhood." But that's not the case. Janice and Jerry Trecker have been supporters, readers, editors, boosters and good friends, too. Not many of my friends can say that they actually like their parents, so I know how lucky I am. Both of them are talented writers in their own right (please buy books written by "Janice Law") and both of them set down their own projects to help get this one done.

George Vecsey and his wife, Marianne, joined us in Berlin and were invaluable. If I could be one-quarter the writer he is, I'd be lucky. Chris Cowles shared flights, trains, interviews, information, and many, many awful matches with me, which probably also earns his lovely wife, Theresa, a thanks as well. Grahame Jones, Amy Lawrence, Kevin McCarra, and Paddy Barclay have all served as sounding boards over the years and led by example. Mac Nwulu, Marcelo Balboa, Derek Rae, and Dave O'Brien all generously gave their time and assistance to me. (Dave and Derek: Don't give up.)

The Dempsey Brothers, Ryan and Clint, kindly made their time and opinions available, as did Carie Goldberg and Richard Motzkin of Wasserman. Jim Trecker helped with his reminiscences of the NASL days as did Clive Toye, Phil Woosnam, Dan Davies and the late Ahmet Ertegün.

Heather Mitchell of Gatorade/Quaker introduced me to invaluable folks like River Plate's Francis Holoway. Dave Clarke of Quinnipiac and Ray Reid of the University of Connecticut took time to chat with me about all matters great and small. Ed Derse, Dermot McQuarrie, and Robert Burns at Fox Sports made sure I was there in the first place and Oliver Hinz was the German expert and translator. Ms. Lynne Truss helped me out more than she knows; the same must be said of Claire Bigley and the Melvins, an aggregation Ms. Bigley will particularly enjoy being grouped beside.

Lisa Fishering's steadfast support was vital during some particularly dark hours shuttling back and forth between doctors; the same is true for Miss Hannah Aitchison (please buy her artwork). Timo and Erik Liekoski; Keith, Taz, Harleigh and Ellen Perry; Daphne Gottlieb (please buy her books, too); Crissy, David, Izzy, Olivia Bernstein, and Heidi Peck: Thanks.

Eric Graf provided the tech, and he and the SG Mac Group provided the tech support. Vicki Hospodka graciously allowed me to drag her husband, John, across five countries in seven days. For this, John read this whole damn thing before you did, and was the "managing editor" of it, forcing me to be better at every turn.

I would be remiss if I did not thank Lawrence Bernstein, MD, and Mardee Stecker (Northwestern); David Edelberg, MD, and Mary Nagle (Whole Health Chicago); and Cyberonics, without whom this book—quite literally—would never have come to pass.

There are a number of people at the team, league, Federation, and FIFA levels who I would thank publicly, but I am positive they do not want their bosses to know they talk to me. They know who they are. To them: Thank you, and I greatly appreciate all of your information and candor.

Last yet not least is Amanda Lifvendahl: Like Li, she read all this, ferried me back and forth to doctors and planes, took time off her grueling work schedule to make sure I was upright, and has helped Li and me out through thin, thinner and thinnest times. Thanks, Panda.

SELECTED BIBLIOGRAPHY

ON GERMANY AND WORLD WAR II

Alter, Reinhard, and Peter Monteath, eds. *Rewriting the German Past: History and Identity in the New Germany.* New Jersey: Humanities Press International, 1997.

Buruma, Ian. "Weimar Faces." *New York Review of Books,* November 2, 2006, 14–18.

Funder, Anna. *Stasiland: True Stories from Behind the Berlin Wall.* London: Granta Books, 2003.

Garfield, Simon. *Our Hidden Lives: The Everyday Diaries of Yesterday's Britain.* London: Ebury Press, 2005.

[Hillers, Marta]. *A Woman in Berlin: Eight Weeks in the Conquered City.* 1954. Reprint, trans. Philip Boehm. New York: Metropolitan Books, 2005.

Ladd, Brian. *The Ghosts of Berlin: Confronting German History in the Urban Landscape.* Chicago: University of Chicago Press, 1997.

Large, David Clay. *Where Ghosts Walked: Munich's Road to the Third Reich.* New York: W. W. Norton, 1996.

Rosenfeld, Gavriel D. *Munich and Memory: Architecture, Monuments, and the Legacy of the Third Reich.* 2000. Reprint, Berkeley, CA: University of California Press, 2006.

Shirer, William L. *The Rise and Fall of the Third Reich: A History of Nazi Germany.* New York: Simon and Schuster, 1960.

Speer, Albert. *Inside the Third Reich.* New York: Galahad, 1970.

Stern, Fritz. *Five Germanys I Have Known.* New York: Farrar, Straus and Giroux, 2006.

Taylor, Ronald. *Berlin and Its Culture: A Historical Portrait.* New Haven, CT: Yale University Press, 1997.

Walters, Guy. *Berlin Games: How the Nazis Stole the Olympic Dream.* New York: William Morrow, 2006.

ON PARIS AND OTHER CITIES

Alter, Robert. *Imagined Cities: Urban Experience and the Language of the Novel.* New Haven, CT: Yale University Press, 2005.

Anderson, Benedict. *Imagined Communities: Reflections on the Origin and Spread of Nationalism.* Rev. ed. London: Verso, 1991.

Cobb, Richard. *Paris and Elsewhere.* Preface by Julian Barnes. New York: NYRB Classics, 2004.

Davis, Mike. *Dead Cities.* New York: New Press, 2002.

———. *Planet of Slums.* London: Verso, 2006.

Hussey, Andrew. *Paris: The Secret History.* London: Bloomsbury, 2006.

Neuwirth, Robert. *Shadow Cities: A Billion Squatters, a New Urban World.* London: Routledge, 2004.

Orwell, George. *Down and Out in Paris and London.* (1930). Reprint. New York: NYR Books, 2005.

Sinclair, Iain. *London Orbital.* 2002. Reprint, London: Penguin Books, 2003.

ON FOOTBALL, FIFA, AND SPORTS

Brown, Adam. *Fanatics: Power, Identity and Fandom in Football.* London: Routledge, 1998.

Buford, Bill. *Among the Thugs.* 1992. Reprint, New York: Vintage, 1993.

Fuller, Stuart. *Fuller's Fans Guide to German Stadiums.* Stuart Fuller, 2005.

Hugman, Barry J., ed. *The PFA Premier and Football League Players' Records, 1946–2005.* London: Queen Anne Press, 2005.

Jennings, Andrew. *Foul! The Secret World of FIFA: Bribes, Vote Rigging and Ticket Scandals.* London: HarperSport, 2006.

Keohane, Mark. *Springbok Rugby Uncovered.* Cape Town: Zebra Press, 2004.

Mazwai, Thami. *Thirty Years of South African Soccer.* 2003. Reprint, Johannesburg: Sunbird, 2004.

McGinniss, Joe. *The Miracle of Castel Di Sangro.* 1999. Reprint, New York: Broadway, 2000.

Oliver, Guy, ed. *Almanack of World Football 2007.* London: Headline Book Publishing, 2006, 2007.

Rollin, Jack, and Glenda Rollin, eds. *Sky Sports Football Yearbook, 2005–2006.* London: Hodder Headline Book Publishing, 2005, 2006.

Sugden, John, and Alan Tomlinson. *Badfellas: FIFA Family at War.* Edinburgh: Mainstream, 2003.

Toye, Clive. *A Kick in the Grass.* Haworth, NJ: Saint Johann Press, 2006.

ON MASS MEDIA

Brewer, John. "Selling the American Way." *New York Review of Books,* November 30, 2006.

De Certeau, Michel. *The Practice of Everyday Life.* 1984. Reprint, Berkeley, CA: University of California Press, 1988.

De Grazia, Victoria. *Irresistible Empire: America's Advance through Twentieth-Century Europe.* Cambridge, MA: Belknap/Harvard University Press, 2006.

Debord, Guy. *Comments on the Society of the Spectacle.* London: Routledge, 1994.

———. *The Society of the Spectacle.* London: Routledge, 1994.

Ehrenreich, Barbara. *Dancing in the Streets: A History of Collective Joy.* New York: Metropolitan Books, 2007.

McLuhan, Marshall. *The Medium Is the Message.* New York: Bantam, 1967.

APPENDIX

FIFA WORLD CUP 2006—SCHEDULE OF GAMES

FIRST ROUND

JUNE 9
Opening ceremony
Germany struggles but beats Costa Rica in Munich opener
(GER 4, CRC 2)
Poland loses to Ecuador at Gelsenkirschen (POL 0, ECU 2)

JUNE 10
England struggles against Paraguay (ENG 1, PAR 0)
Trinidad and Tobago holds Sweden to draw (SWE 0, TRI 0)
Argentina shades Ivory Coast (ARG 2, CIV 1)

JUNE 11
Dutch beat Serbia and Montenegro in Leipzig (NED 1, SCG 0)
Angola gives former colonists Portugal a scare (POR 1, ANG 0)
Mexico impresses with walloping of Iran (MEX 3, IRN 1)

JUNE 12
USA fails to show up, gets battered by Czech Republic
(USA 0, CZE 3)
Aussies roar past Asian champs Japan (AUS 3, JPN 1)
Italy starts strong with win over Ghana (ITA 2, GHA 0)

JUNE 13

South Korea edges Togo; game overshadowed by strike threats
(KOR 2, TOG 1)

Brazil does just enough to beat Croatia in Berlin (BRA 1, CRO 0)

France stuns onlookers with poor draw against Switzerland
(FRA 0, SUI 0)

JUNE 14

Germans blow away Poles with last-minute goal; game in
Dortmund is marred by pregame violence (GER 1, POL 0)

Spain crushes Ukraine; Ukraine falls to dead last in Cup
(ESP 4, UKR 0)

Late flurry leaves Tunisia and Saudi Arabia all drawn
(TUN 2, KSA 2)

JUNE 15

Peter Crouch helps beat Trinidad and Tobago, but England shaken
(ENG 2, TRI 0)

Ecuador runs over Costa Rica (ECU 3, CRC 0)

Sweden knocks out Paraguay (SWE 1, PAR 0)

JUNE 16

Holland locks up second-round slot with win over Ivory Coast
(NED 2, CIV 1)

Argentina debuts Lionel Messi, massacres Serbia and Montenegro
(ARG 6, SCG 1)

Keeper João Ricardo gains Angola a draw against Mexico
(MEX 0, ANG 0)

JUNE 17

Nine-man USA holds Italy to a draw in stunner (USA 1, ITA 1)

Ghana offs a sluggish Czech team, throws group wide open
(GHA 2, CZE 0)

Portugal routs Iran (POR 2, IRN 0)

JUNE 18

Brazil pins back Aussies at Allianz (BRA 2, AUS 0)

Japan ekes out draw with Croats (JPN 0, CRO 0)

Park Ji-Sung takes the Reds to the top of the group past France (FRA 1, KOR 1)

JUNE 19

Switzerland handles Togo with ease (SUI 2, TOG 0)

Ukraine crushes Saudis (UKR 4, KSA 0)

Spain wallops Tunisia, locks up slot (ESP 3, TUN 1)

After thirty-two games, in straight table, the top teams were Argentina, Brazil, Ecuador, England, Germany, Holland, Portugal, and Spain.

JUNE 20

(Four-a-days start; **bold** indicates qualification for second round)

Germany beats **Ecuador** (GER 3 ECU 0)

England draws **Swedes** (ENG 2, SWE 2)

Paraguay downs plucky T and T (PAR 2, TRI 0)

Poland beats up on hapless Costa Rica (POL 2, CRC 1)

JUNE 21

Holland draws with **Argentina** in snoozer; both already through (NED 0, ARG 0)

Ivory Coast thrills in rain against Serbs (CIV 3, SCG 2)

Portuguese off **Mexico** (POR 2, MEX 1)

Iran draws Angola, does neither team any good (IRN 1, ANG 1)

JUNE 22

Ghana eliminates USA; Dempsey scores lone American goal (GHA 2, USA 1)

Czechs fall to **Italy** (CZE 0, ITA 2)

Brazil sends Japan packing (BRA 4, JPN 0)

Croatia draws **Aussies,** 'Roos slide through (CRO 2, AUS 2)

JUNE 23
Spain edges Saudi Arabia in surprisingly tight game
(ESP 1, KSA 0)
Ukraine beats Tunisia (UKR 1, TUN 0)
France beats Togo to go through (FRA 2, TOG 0)
Swiss beat Tunisia (SUI 2, TUN 0)

SECOND ROUND

JUNE 24
Germany glides past Swedes (GER 2, SWE 0)
Argentina taken to extra time by a plucky Mexico
(ARG 2, MEX 1, AET)

JUNE 25
Holland loses to **Portugal** in ugly game (NED 0, POR 1):
Sixteen yellow cards are issued and four players—two from each
side—are ejected in a vicious match.
England beats Ecuador (ENG 1, ECU 0)

JUNE 26
Ten-man **Italy** gifted late penalty, wins against Aussies
(ITA 1, AUS 0)
Swiss stagger to loss against **Ukraine** on penalty kicks (pks)
(SUI 0, UKR 0; SUI lose 0–3 on pks)

JUNE 27
Brazil crushes outclassed Ghana (BRA 3, GHA 0)
France topples Spain in shocker (ESP 1, FRA 3)

KNOCKOUT ROUND ENDS

JUNE 28 (DAY OFF)

JUNE 29 (DAY OFF)

QUARTERFINALS

JUNE 30
Germany needs kicks to down Argentina (GER 1, ARG 1, 4–2 on pks)
Italy crushes Ukraine (ITA 3, UKR 0)

JULY 1
France ousts Brazil; Thierry Henry scores the goal of the Cup (FRA 1, BRA 0)
England collapses on kicks to **Portugal** (ENG 0, POR 0, 1–3 on pks)

SEMIFINALS

JULY 4
Italy dazzles in overtime to oust hosts (ITA 2, GER 0, AET)

JULY 5
Zidane sinks penalty, **France** sinks Portugal (FRA 1, POR 0)

THIRD PLACE

JULY 8
Germany beats Portugal, hosts take third (GER 3, POR 1)

FINAL

JULY 9 BERLIN
Italy wins Cup on penalty kicks (FRA 1, ITA 1 AET; Italy wins 5–3 on pks)

INDEX